Amazon Cloud Computing With Java

Aditya Yadav

Copyright © 2009 by Aditya Yadav (http://adityayadav.com)

Copyright

Amazon Cloud Computing With Java

Copyright © 2009 by Aditya Yadav

All rights reserved. No part of this work may be reproduced or transmitted in any form or by any means, electronic or mechanical, including photocopying, recording, or by any information storage or retrieval system, without the prior written permission of the copyright owner and the publisher.

ISBN-13: 978-0-557-25527-6

Trademarked names may appear in this book. Rather than use a trademark symbol with every occurrence of a trademarked name, we use the names only in an editorial fashion and to the benefit of the trademark owner, with no intention of infringement of the trademark.

To Baby Alisha Who Has Made Me Realize How Beautiful Life Can Be

Contents

Prepping Up 15

Chapter 1- Amazon EC2 AMI Building 17

    Using the AMI Builder to Build AMI's 39

    Retrospective 45

Chapter 2- Amazon Management Console 46

    Amazon EC2 46

    Amazon Elastic MapReduce 59

    Amazon CloudFront 59

    Retrospective 62

Chapter 3- Writing our own Monitoring Application 63

    Retrospective 66

Chapter 4- Elastic Compute Cloud 67

    Retrospective 69

Chapter 5- Cloud Watch 70

    Using CloudWatch 77

    Retrospective 82

Chapter 6- Elastic Load Balancing & Auto Scaling 83

    Using LoadBalancing & AutoScaling Manager 116

    Retrospective 119

Chapter 7- Simple Storage Service 120

    Using the S3 Manager 137

    Retrospective 139

Copyright © 2009 by Aditya Yadav (http://adityayadav.com)

Chapter 8- Virtual Private Cloud 140

Using VPC Manager 171

Retrospective 177

Chapter 9- SimpleDB 178

Using the SimpleDB Manager 192

Retrospective 194

Chapter 10- Relational Database Service 195

Using RDS Manager 203

Retrospective 206

Chapter 11- Cloud Front 207

Using the CloudFront console application 211

Retrospective 213

Chapter 12- Simple Queue Service 214

Using the SQS Mail application 224

Retrospective 225

Chapter 13- Elastic MapReduce 226

Using MapReduce Manager 244

Retrospective 245

Chapter 14- Agile Continuous Integration with Amazon EC2 using Ant 246

Retrospective 275

Chapter 15-Using Eclipse for AWS Development 276

Configuring AWS Toolkit 276

Create the runtime configuration 278

Create the web application 281

Remote debugging our web application 285

Managing AMI's Instance's etc. 286

Retrospective 288

Foreword

Over the years I have worked with organizations who were never on the cutting edge of technology. The reasons for which were partly the risk involved, partly the knowledge of their leading practitioners, the ambiguity around cutting edge technologies as they evolve, lack of time to follow each development, and lack of a guide they could use to quickly try out the offerings, evaluate and make decisions. This book has been an attempt to answer a lot of how's and why's around cloud computing in general and Amazon Webservices in particular.

During my stint at my p2p startup I realized that being on this side technologists think mostly in terms of breakthroughs while businesses on the other side think mostly in terms of how it solves their problems and issues. This book takes a middle path and tries to cover both by illustrating what's involved in developing applications for Amazon Webservices. We chose Java because of the sheer number of Java developers, systems and codebase. Java is extensively deployed on the server. We will be building a dozen odd small applications which will double as AWS management tools.

Initiating an effort to cloud-ify enterprise applications is as much a business decision as a technical decision. I think I have been able to demonstrate to people that there is nothing like a cloud standard, and the issues of lock-in still remain. With the examples presented in this book we will be able to isolate Amazon specific code modularly. Sometimes porting an application to the cloud will still require a complete reengineering of the application and with this book architects and technical leaders will be able to understand and estimate the effort better.

I also believe that the two most important groups interested in the cloud are ones who occasionally need a lot of compute power and the startups who want to pay as they go and not invest in heavy infrastructure upfront. The first group is mostly interested in the problem domain and wants to stay away from the details of the platform. While the latter would like to concentrate on developing their business rather than worrying about the platform. I believe both the groups would be able to judge the merits of the Amazon Webservices platform in the context of their business needs. I hope to see a lot more startups running off the Amazon cloud infrastructure. Over the years I have learnt that business is not about technology but it's about solutions. And even though this book is pretty techie it is meant to answer the one big question "What is the Amazon Webservices Platform and how do we leverage it for our business" While you go through this book just sit back every once in a while and think how the information presented would help you create better solutions to business problems in your company/industry. I think I would like to look at technology through those eyes.

ADITYA YADAV

Preface

In 2005-6 I started working on projects that used virtualized infrastructures with some sort of dynamic provisioning. The real Cloud projects started coming in by late 2008 and it was very difficult for me to spend over a month getting the team upto speed with Cloud Computing concepts and helping them adopt the new paradigm in their applications. While the corporate directives were there to pilot such applications. Delivering them was beginning to be a challenge. And I started taking down notes & how-to documents which I used to send across to my team mates when they encountered problems.

I realized that if I have to effectively deliver such projects with my team we needed crash courses in Cloud Computing, something which was comprehensive and yet very light weight to help teams get started. Which led to Bootcamps and Learn-As-You-Do lunch sessions. By the beginning of 2009 so many teams adopted AWS that it was practically infeasible for me or any one group of coach's to scale such that they could help teams of 100 engineers or more.

This finally led to the writing of this book which is intended as a single weekend crash course for engineers, architects and leaders to learn what AWS is all about and how to plan, migrate, and deliver applications using it.

In 2009 end I decided to convert this rough book into a production quality book so that it could benefit a worldwide audience. And that is when I came across the editors who agreed with this idea and helped me convert my rough notes into a production quality book. What you read in the following chapters are tried and tested examples which work, and you will get the source code to all of them. I hope with this book it will be the best weekend you will invest in learning AWS.

ADITYA YADAV

Copyright © 2009 by Aditya Yadav (http://adityayadav.com)

Acknowledgements

Writing this book has been an exciting journey that brought several incredible people together to support me. I would like to thank the knowledgeable reviewers for some of the best feedback during the writing of this book. The advice included which topics were most important to them and from general observations in the industry wide pilot adoptions. I would like to thank people at Thoughtworks, my former employer, who helped me make up my mind to write this book.

I took a 4 month sabbatical from work to embark on this journey which has been very fulfilling in many ways. I would like to thank my father Jai Raj Yadav who financially supported me through the sabbatical and with all the resources, travel, household, loan payments and other expenses. Leaving me free to concentrate on nothing but writing the book. I would like to thank my wife Renu for her undivided support during these 4 months. We are expecting a kid in Feb 2009 and it has been hard on Renu to leave me alone for long hours undisturbed. She always remembered to serve tea to me every 2 hours all throughout this time, with a smile, I hope I have lived upto her expectations. My 3 year old daughter The Alisha Monster attacks the computer every now and then asking me to show her Disney movies but somehow she has abstained so far. I would like to thank my brother and sister in law Amit and Kalpana, and my mother R.D. Yadav for their faith in me.

I would like to thank the editors who painstakingly proofread the book and the publishers who were all the way through this journey. It is with their help we could together convert a raw idea into a production quality book.

Copyright © 2009 by Aditya Yadav (http://adityayadav.com)

About this book

You may be wondering if there is the need for another book on Amazon Web Services. I have been using AWS for the last 2-3 odd years and have watched it grow into the leader it is today. While I'm impressed by the offerings often when I suggest Amazon Web Services to my clients or on my projects, I get a look 'Isn't that complicated and tough', 'How do we learn so much?' and 'Can we do all this and still make our project timelines?' I haven't found a single book (I look primarily at Amazon.com and local book stores) which comprehensively covers all the AWS offerings. AWS is quite complicated to get started with. And leaders don't know how to plan for it and what to expect. While there are other issues like Reliability, Security and other Compliances which leaders and architects need to worry about which I don't cover in this book.

I wrote this book to help readers get started with AWS by spending one weekend and less than $20 on AWS costs learning it. Also AWS has a very limited management console and during the excercises in this book we walk through all the API's and how to use them. The examples also double as effective AWS management tools making the purchase of expensive third party management softwares and tools redundant.

I'm an agile coach and everything I do or look at, I look at through my agile lenses. And that's why in this book I have covered some agile techniques, primarily countinous integration and automated functional testing with EC2. Which is something I do on all my projects whether ones on the cloud or in the enterprise. I'm sure this will attract many agile purists. Who will be able to extend their practices into this new environment.

Cloud adoption is not a straightforward process. And many things need to be planned including but not limited to the actual changes to the software systems. Some of those concerns are around Vendor lock-ins. With this book I'm sure the readers will be able to plan and isolate AWS specific functionality. AWS doesn't provide a local sandbox environment but most of Amazon specific functionality can also be accessed from the developer's machines.

Copyright © 2009 by Aditya Yadav (http://adityayadav.com)

The other thing I would like to point out is 'AWS instance leaks'. By which I mean, I have observed in my past projects where multiple developers are developing modules over AWS that they start instances and sooner or later nobody knows who owns which instances. Whether they forgot to shut them down and they are no longer needed. That's one of the reasons I put in a sample chapter on AWS Monitor which otherwise seems primitive compared to the rest of the excercises but has very high relevance in a practical project. The readers need to extend it to suite their needs. And probably expose the AWS Monitor in full screen mode on a centrally located desktop which the whole team can see.

I'm sure my readers don't plan to use just EC2 or just SQS. This book will get them started with all of the AWS cloud offerings so that they will be able to define, plan and build real life solutions.

Roadmap

Prepping Up outlines all the resources that are at your disposal as you go through this book and work on AWS projects.

Chapter 1 discusses Amazon EC2 AMI Building. It will walk the users through the activities that involve launching instances from available AMI's and then modifying them, bundling them and registering them as AMI's.

Chapter 2 introduces the Amazon Management Console and covers EC2 management, and CloudFront management, while Elastic MapReduce management is covered in detail in its own chapter.

Chapter 3 walks the reader through building an AWS monitoring application which they can extend and use on their projects.

Chapter 4 discusses EC2. AWS is centered on EC2 so this chapter summarizes what EC2 is all about while it is amply covered through the other chapters in this book.

Chapter 5 discusses CloudWatch which is a mechanism to monitor AWS resources.

Chapter 6 talks about Elastic LoadBalancing and AutoScaling which are normally meant to work together. It will walk the readers through setting up a LoadBalancer and AutoScaling with auto-provisioning & de-provisioning of instances as the Measures vary and Triggers get fired.

Chapter 7 focuses on S3 which is a simple storage to store objects in buckets. These buckets can be used to store AMI's, MapReduce inputs, outputs, logs and programs, CloudFront files or application data.

Chapter 8 talks about how to setup a Virtual Private Cloud composed of AWS resources and your enterprise appliances such that they all work uniformly with corporate DHCP, Firewalls and policies.

Chapter 9 focuses on SimpleDB and shows how it can be used to store Items with arbitrary attributes, queried using an SQL like syntax.

Chapter 10 focuses on RDS which is a modified MySQL service which can be utilized by your applications without worrying about scalability or extensive administration, using the regular MySQL tools you are already familiar with.

Chapter 11 discusses CloudFront which is a CDN that you can configure to serve files from your bucket utilizing Amazon edge servers spread throughout the world.

Chapter 12 covers SQS which is a point to point scalable messaging Queue implementation.

Chapter 13 covers Elastic MapReduce which is a customization of Hadoop running on Amazon on Debian 5.0, to run arbitrary programs as Mappers and Reducers using streaming.

Chapter 14 talks about how we can setup continous integration with EC2 and run our CI integrated automated functional tests on it, which is one of the most important agile practices.

Chapter 15 walks the user through configuring the Eclipse AWS Toolkit, creating a small web application with it, running and debugging it on AWS.

Copyright © 2009 by Aditya Yadav (http://adityayadav.com)

Author Online

The resources for this book can be found and the author can be reached at http://adityayadav.com. You can download the source code accompanying this book at the above website, and also access the errata. The above website will be accessible as long as the book is in print. Please try the Amazon Webservices Developer Community Forums http://developer.amazonwebservices.com/. If the question still remains unanswered please send it to the author through the author's website. The author will answer the questions and also post them on the website for everyone to see. Though this is not a commitment on the part of the author as his contributions to the forum and email responses remain voluntary (and unpaid).

The author has been the CTO of one of the top 25 startups in India dealing with global scale real-time multimedia P2P products. He is also a technology and technology strategy consultant to fortune companies; he provides leadership coaching and architects world class engineering organizations for his clients. He can be reached even outside the context of this book through the author's website.

Prepping Up

For the purpose of this book we will run all the exercises on Windows XP, but Windows Vista or Windows 7 would also do. The first step is to install JDK1.5; the libraries we are using have conflicts with the JDK 1.6 library versions. The AWS Toolkit for Eclipse website is at http://aws.amazon.com/eclipse/

Download and install 'Eclipse IDE for Java EE Developers 3.4', download the Eclipse Data Tools Platform from http://www.eclipse.org/downloads/download.php?file=/datatools/downloads/1.7/dtp-sdk_1.7.0.zip extract it and merge its features and plugins directory with the installed eclipse's features and plugins directories and restart eclipse. Then use the eclipse ide update from http://aws.amazon.com/eclipse/ to get the AWS Toolkit for eclipse. Restart Eclipse.

It will be a good time to download the Source Code accompanying this book from http://adityayadav.com, we will just be illustrating the essential pieces of the programs and not list the complete program, for which you have to refer to the Source Code bundle. Also you will be able to create your applications with the projects in the bundle as starting points. We have used JFormDesigner to design the Swing Forms in the bundle, you can download a 20 day evaluation of the plugin from http://www.formdev.com/ extract it and merge its features and plugins directories with eclipse's and restart eclipse.

Download the windows installer for Putty from http://www.chiark.greenend.org.uk/~sgtatham/putty/download.html it has a name similar to putty-0.60-installer.exe install it into the default location on windows. We are going to use it along with eclipse and AWS Toolkit in the last chapter.

The last step is to use your credit card to register for Amazon Web Services http://aws.amazon.com/ after you are done you have to goto http://aws.amazon.com/security-credentials and note down the following.

Copyright © 2009 by Aditya Yadav (http://adityayadav.com)

Access Key ID (For example: 022QF06E7MXBSH9DHM02)

Secret Access Key (For example: kWcrlUX5JEDGM/LtmEENI/aVmYvHNif5zB+d9+ct)

You will have to enter this in the programs configuration files. Without which the programs won't work. This will link the program to your Amazon account and you will be charged depending on your service usage. We have spent less than US$20 in developing all the exercises and you should expect a similar figure doing them. Please remember to turn off all instances on the cloud and stop the programs to avoid running charges, when you are done. Even if, not explicitly mentioned in the book. Total time to cover the whole book going through all the exercise's is approximately 16 hours over one weekend, assuming you go through the exercise's in the book and use the book source code to run the exercises along with some modifications and self learning.

Even though you have an AWS account you will have to signup for each of the products you want to use on the portal. We will do that when we come to trying out each of the products in each chapter. Further Documentation, sample code, articles, tutorials, and more can be found in the AWS Resource Center: http://aws.amazon.com/resources/. Amazon management console can be accessed at http://aws.amazon.com/console/ and developer tools can be downloaded or accessed from http://developer.amazonwebservices.com/connect/kbcategory.jspa?categoryID=88. The webpage for Java development on Amazon Cloud is located at http://aws.amazon.com/java/ and the API documentation can be found at http://aws.amazon.com/documentation/.

Basic proficiency in using Windows, Eclipse and developing Java/Swing programs is assumed by the author. The book will not show clips of basic steps which are done even otherwise while developing enterprise Java/Swing applications, we will try to illustrate only that is specific to AWS development.

Chapter 1- Amazon EC2 AMI Building

The Amazon Java Library wraps the complete API to Amazon EC2 amongst other services and in this chapter we will build a small Swing application to create a Windows AMI for us from one of the Windows AMI Images available at Amazon. This would be a good time to register for EC2 and S3 with your Amazon account. You will need access to a phone with incoming enabled to verify your account. Amazon has a concept of AMI's or Amazon Machine Images. If you have used Virtualization tools like VirtualBox or VMWare this is something like virtual machines. AMI's are stored on EBS or S3. These are different kinds of systems. S3 is a general purpose storage which stores data in buckets while EBS is specifically meant for AMI's and uses the concept of Volumes and Snapshots. A volume is a virtual hard disk while a snapshot is a photo/snapshot of a running system. Both can be used to create instances of virtual machines. S3 for our purpose here will be used to store AMI's but can store anything for that matter. The AMI Builder software developed here will illustrate the API's used so that you can create programs to automate AMI Building maybe through Ant build files or through a Eclipse Plugin if you may.

We are going to make an application which will help us make Instance-Store (S3) AMI's, we will be able to create an instance from an AMI, run it, get access to it through Windows Remote Desktop, make some changes and Bundle it back again into an AMI and store it in S3 and register it as an AMI which we can use later if required. But for the purpose of this exercise terminate all instances and delete all bundles from S3 when you are done using the chapter. They incur a recurring time based cost. So even if not mentioned please terminate and delete all instances and S3 buckets if you take a long break or are done with this chapter.

For the purpose of this exercise please login to the Amazon Management Console for EC2 at https://console.aws.amazon.com/ec2/home. You can learn more about the Amazon Management Console in the chapter by that name in this book.

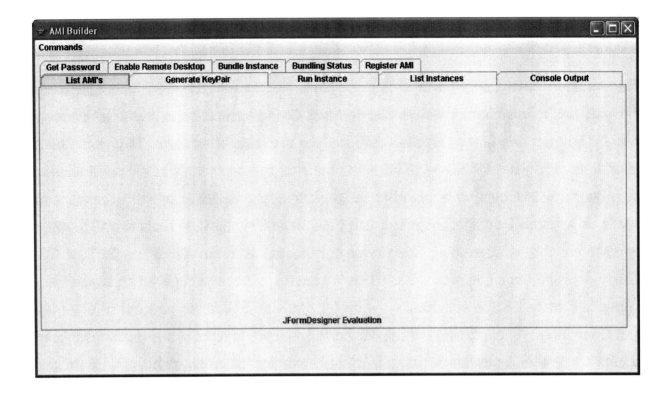

Figure 1 - Finished AMI Builder Application

The file name for the application form is com.ayny.application.AMIBuilder. It has the following menu items.

1. List AMI's
2. Generate KeyPair
3. Run Instance
4. List Instances
5. Console Output
6. Get Password
7. Enable Remote Desktop
8. Bundle Instance
9. Bundling Status
10. Register AMI
11. Exit

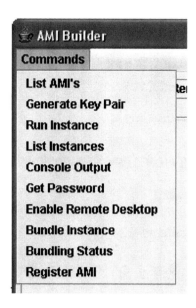

Figure 2 - AMI Builder Menu Structure

Now let's see what the List AMI's event handler code is like. The list ami's tab page contains one JTable.

List AMIs event handler code

```
private class ListAMIs extends AbstractAction {

        private ListAMIs() {

                // JFormDesigner - Action initialization - DO NOT MODIFY    //GEN-BEGIN:initComponents

                // Generated using JFormDesigner Evaluation license - Aditya Yadav

                putValue(NAME, "List AMI's");

                // JFormDesigner - End of action initialization  //GEN-END:initComponents

        }


        public void actionPerformed(ActionEvent e) {

                try
```

```java
        {
            AmazonEC2Client ec2 = AmazonClientFactory.getInstance().getEC2Client();

            DescribeImagesRequest request = new DescribeImagesRequest();

            request.getOwner().add("self");

            request.getOwner().add("amazon");

            DescribeImagesResponse response = ec2.describeImages(request);

            Object[] columnIdentifiers = new Object[]{"Image Id", "Root Device Type", "Owner Id", "Image Owner Alias","Image Location","Image Type","Visibility","Platform","Architecture", "Description" };


            ArrayList data = new ArrayList();

            for (Image image : response.getDescribeImagesResult().getImage())

            {

                data.add(new Object[]{image.getImageId(),image.getRootDeviceType(),image.getOwnerId(),image.getImageOwnerAlias(),image.getImageLocation(),image.getImageType(),image.getVisibility(),image.getPlatform(),image.getArchitecture(),image.getDescription()});

            }

            DefaultTableModel tableModel = (DefaultTableModel)tablelistAMIs.getModel();

            tableModel.setDataVector((Object[][])data.toArray(new Object[0][0]), columnIdentifiers);

            JOptionPane.showMessageDialog(AMIBuilder.this,"List AMIs Completed. ");

        }

        catch (Exception ex)
```

```
            {
                JOptionPane.showMessageDialog(AMIBuilder.this,"Error Executing List AMIs. " +
ex.getMessage());
            }
        }
    }
```

The list AMIs method makes a describe images request and loops over a list of images, gets the ami attributes and populates the table. It uses 2 filters which show only AMIs owned by the user or Amazon. Lets look at the generate key pair tab page. The Generate key pair tab page looks like shown below.

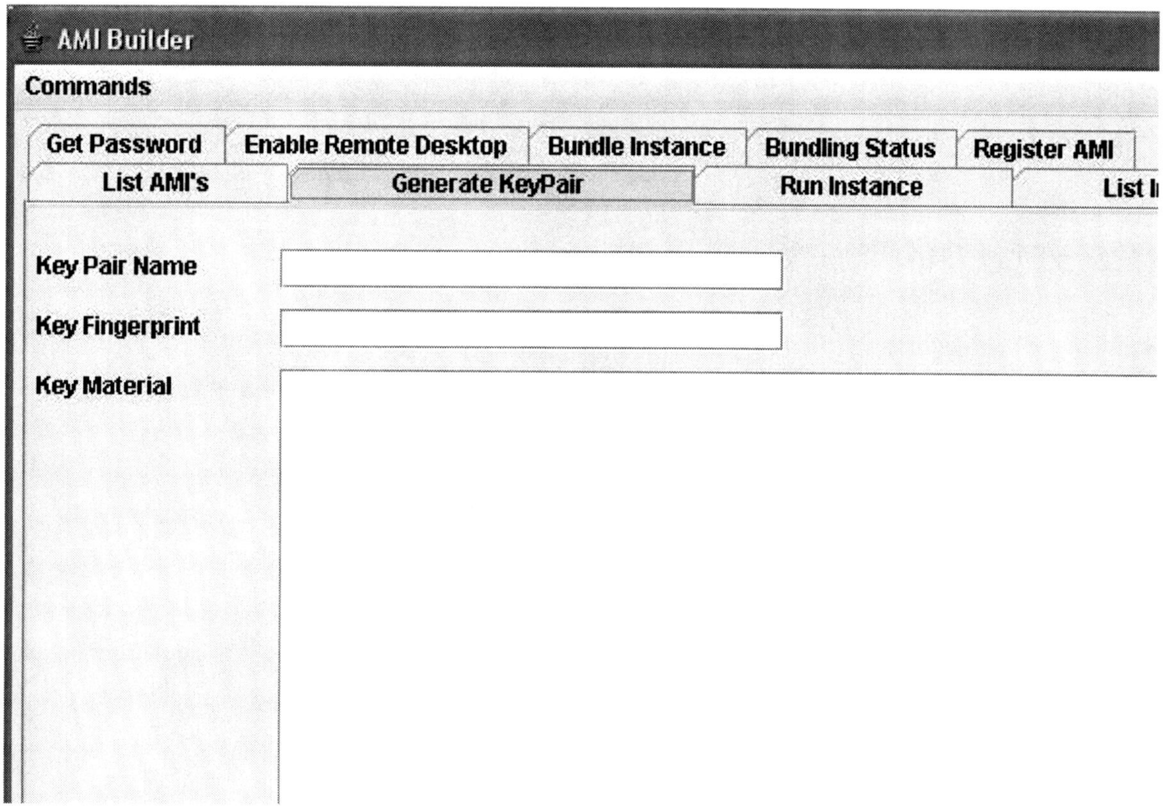

Figure 3 - Generate Key Pair Tab Page

Generate Key Pair event handler code

```java
private class GenerateKeyPair extends AbstractAction {

    private GenerateKeyPair() {
        // JFormDesigner - Action initialization - DO NOT MODIFY  //GEN-BEGIN:initComponents
        // Generated using JFormDesigner Evaluation license - Aditya Yadav
        putValue(NAME, "Generate Key Pair");
        // JFormDesigner - End of action initialization  //GEN-END:initComponents
    }


    public void actionPerformed(ActionEvent e) {
        try
        {
            AmazonEC2Client ec2 = AmazonClientFactory.getInstance().getEC2Client();

            CreateKeyPairRequest request = new CreateKeyPairRequest();
            request.setKeyName(textFieldKeyPairName.getText());
            CreateKeyPairResponse response = ec2.createKeyPair(request);

            textFieldKeyFingerPrint.setText(response.getCreateKeyPairResult().getKeyPair().getKeyFingerprint());

            textPaneKeyMaterial.setText(response.getCreateKeyPairResult().getKeyPair().getKeyMaterial());
```

```java
        FileOutputStream fos = new FileOutputStream(textFieldKeyPairName.getText()+".key");

        fos.write(response.getCreateKeyPairResult().getKeyPair().getKeyMaterial().getBytes());

        fos.close();

            JOptionPane.showMessageDialog(AMIBuilder.this,"Generate Key Pair Completed.");

        }

        catch (Exception ex)
        {
            JOptionPane.showMessageDialog(AMIBuilder.this,"Error Executing Generate KeyPair." + ex.getMessage());
        }
        }
    }
```

The above method makes a generate key pair request and updates the display with Key Fingerprint and Material. It also stores the key into a file with the name <KeyPairName>.key. Let's look at the Run Instance method. The Run Instance Tab Page looks like as shown below.

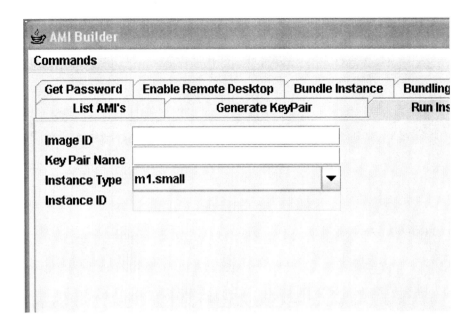

Figure 4 - Run Instance Tab Page

```
Run Instance event handler code

private class RunInstance extends AbstractAction {

        private RunInstance() {

                // JFormDesigner - Action initialization - DO NOT MODIFY    //GEN-BEGIN:initComponents

                // Generated using JFormDesigner Evaluation license - Aditya Yadav

                putValue(NAME, "Run Instance");

                // JFormDesigner - End of action initialization  //GEN-END:initComponents

        }


        public void actionPerformed(ActionEvent e) {

                try
        {
                                AmazonEC2Client            ec2            =
```

```
AmazonClientFactory.getInstance().getEC2Client();


        RunInstancesRequest request = new RunInstancesRequest();

    request.setImageId(textFieldRunInstanceImageId.getText());

    request.setKeyName(textFieldRunInstanceKeyPairName.getText());

    request.setMinCount(1);

    request.setMaxCount(1);

    MonitoringSpecification mSpec = new MonitoringSpecification();

    mSpec.setEnabled(true);

    request.setMonitoring(mSpec);

    request.getSecurityGroup().add("default");

    request.setInstanceType((String)
comboBoxRunInstanceInstanceType.getSelectedItem());

    RunInstancesResponse response = ec2.runInstances(request);

textFieldRunInstanceInstanceID.setText(response.getRunInstancesResult().getReservation().getRunningInstance().get(0).getInstanceId());

        JOptionPane.showMessageDialog(AMIBuilder.this,"Run Instance Completed. ");

    }

    catch (Exception ex)

    {

        JOptionPane.showMessageDialog(AMIBuilder.this,"Error Executing Run Instance." + ex.getMessage());

    }
  }
```

```
        }
```

The above method runs an instance with the given AMI Image Id, min and max number of instances as 1, enables monitoring, and adds the instance to the 'default' security group. Let's look at the List Instances Tab Page, it has one JTable in it.

List Instances event handler code

```java
private class ListInstances extends AbstractAction {

        private ListInstances() {

                // JFormDesigner - Action initialization - DO NOT MODIFY  //GEN-BEGIN:initComponents

                // Generated using JFormDesigner Evaluation license - Aditya Yadav

                putValue(NAME, "List Instances");

                // JFormDesigner - End of action initialization  //GEN-END:initComponents

        }


        public void actionPerformed(ActionEvent e) {

                try
        {

                        AmazonEC2Client ec2 = AmazonClientFactory.getInstance().getEC2Client();

                        DescribeInstancesRequest request = new DescribeInstancesRequest();

                        DescribeInstancesResponse response = ec2.describeInstances(request);

                        Object[] columnIdentifiers = new Object[]{"Owner Id","Requester Id","Reservation
```

```java
Id","Image Id","Instance Id","State","Instance Type","IP Address","Public DNS" };

            ArrayList data = new ArrayList();
    for (Reservation reservation : response.getDescribeInstancesResult().getReservation())
        {
            for (RunningInstance runningInstance: reservation.getRunningInstance()){
                data.add(new                  Object[]{reservation.getOwnerId(),
reservation.getRequesterId(),    reservation.getReservationId(),    runningInstance.getImageId(),
runningInstance.getInstanceId(),
runningInstance.getInstanceState(),runningInstance.getInstanceType(),
runningInstance.getIpAddress(), runningInstance.getPublicDnsName()});
            }
        }
        DefaultTableModel tableModel = (DefaultTableModel)tableListInstances.getModel();
        tableModel.setDataVector((Object[][])data.toArray(new Object[0][0]), columnIdentifiers);
            JOptionPane.showMessageDialog(AMIBuilder.this,"List Instances Completed. ");
        }
        catch (Exception ex)
        {
            JOptionPane.showMessageDialog(AMIBuilder.this,"Error Executing List Instances. " + ex.getMessage());
        }
            }
        }
```

The above code makes a describe instances request and updates the jtable with the details from each of the instances returned. Let's look at the Console Output Tab Page as shown below

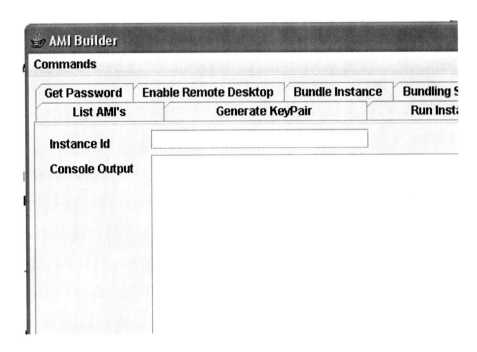

Figure 5 - Console Output Tab Page

```
Console Output event handler code
```

```java
private class ConsoleOutput extends AbstractAction {

    private ConsoleOutput() {

        // JFormDesigner - Action initialization - DO NOT MODIFY  //GEN-BEGIN:initComponents

        // Generated using JFormDesigner Evaluation license - Aditya Yadav

        putValue(NAME, "Console Output");

        // JFormDesigner - End of action initialization  //GEN-END:initComponents

    }



    public void actionPerformed(ActionEvent e) {
```

```java
                try
        {
                        AmazonEC2Client                ec2                =
AmazonClientFactory.getInstance().getEC2Client();


        GetConsoleOutputRequest request = new GetConsoleOutputRequest();

        request.setInstanceId(textFieldConsoleOutputInstanceId.getText());

        GetConsoleOutputResponse response = ec2.getConsoleOutput(request);

        if  (response.getGetConsoleOutputResult().getConsoleOutput().getOutput() != null &&
!response.getGetConsoleOutputResult().getConsoleOutput().getOutput().trim().equals(""))

        {

textPaneConsoleOutput.setText(Base64Coder.decodeString(response.getGetConsoleOutputResult().getConsoleOutput().getOutput()));

        }
            JOptionPane.showMessageDialog(AMIBuilder.this,"Console Output Completed. ");
        }
        catch (Exception ex)
        {
            JOptionPane.showMessageDialog(AMIBuilder.this,"Error    Executing    Console
Output." + ex.getMessage());
        }
            }
        }
```

The above code makes a call to get the console output which is base 64 coded so it decodes it and displays it on the screen. Let's look at the Get Password Tab Page as shown below.

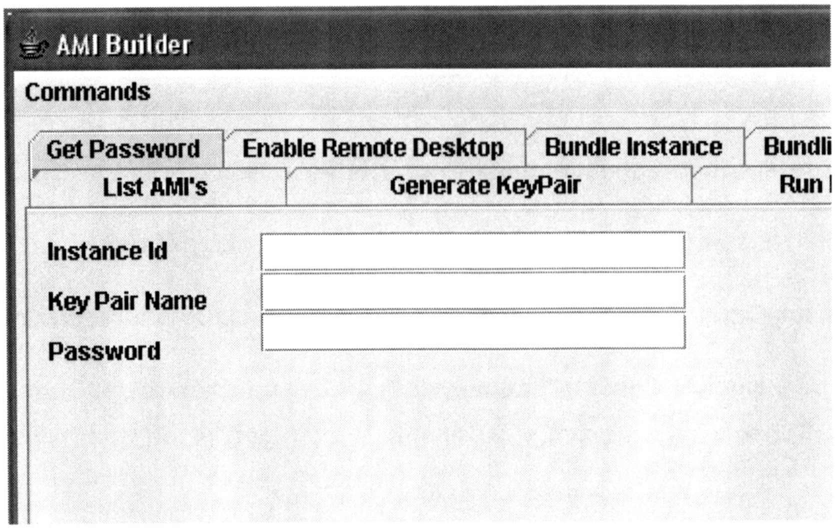

Figure 6 - Get Password Tab Page

Get Password event handler code & helpers

```
private class GetPassword extends AbstractAction {
            private GetPassword() {
                // JFormDesigner - Action initialization - DO NOT MODIFY
                // //GEN-BEGIN:initComponents
                // Generated using JFormDesigner Evaluation license - Aditya Yadav
                putValue(NAME, "Get Password");
                // JFormDesigner - End of action initialization
                // //GEN-END:initComponents
            }

            public void actionPerformed(ActionEvent e) {
                try {
                            AmazonEC2Client ec2 = AmazonClientFactory.getInstance()
                                        .getEC2Client();

                            GetPasswordDataRequest request = new GetPasswordDataRequest();
                            request.setInstanceId(textFieldGetPasswordInstanceId.getText());

                            GetPasswordDataResponse response = ec2.getPasswordData(request);
                            if (response.getGetPasswordDataResult().getPasswordData().getData() != null
                                        &&
                            !response.getGetPasswordDataResult().getPasswordData().getData().trim().equals("")) {
```

```java
                    byte[] temp =
Base64.decodeBase64(response.getGetPasswordDataResult().getPasswordData().getData().getBytes());

            textFieldGetPasswordPassword.setText(decryptData(temp,textFieldGetPasswordKeyPairName.getText()+ ".key"));

                }
                JOptionPane.showMessageDialog(AMIBuilder.this,
                        "Get Password Completed. ");
            } catch (Exception ex) {
                JOptionPane.showMessageDialog(AMIBuilder.this,
                        "Error Executing Get Password." + ex.getMessage());
                ex.printStackTrace();
            }
        }
    }

    public static String decryptData(byte data[], String keyfile)
            throws Exception {
        PrivateKey privateKey;
        try {
            privateKey = getKeyFromFile(keyfile);
        } catch (Exception e) {
            throw new RuntimeException("Error reading private key", e);
        }
        Cipher c = Cipher.getInstance("RSA/ECB/PKCS1Padding");
        c.init(2, privateKey);
        //byte[] outbuf = new byte[c.getOutputSize(data.length)];
        //int outlen = c.update(data, 0, data.length, outbuf);
        c.update(data);
        return new String(c.doFinal());

        //return new String(outbuf,0,outlen);
    }

    public static PrivateKey getKeyFromFile(String keyfile) throws Exception {
        BufferedReader br = new BufferedReader(new FileReader(keyfile));
        StringBuffer keyBuf = new StringBuffer();
        do {
            String line;
            if ((line = br.readLine()) == null) {
                break;
            }
            if (!line.startsWith("-----BEGIN") && !line.startsWith("-----END")) {
                keyBuf.append(line);
                keyBuf.append("\n");
            }
        } while (true);
        br.close();
        PKCS8EncodedKeySpec privKeySpec = new PKCS8EncodedKeySpec(Base64.decodeBase64(keyBuf.toString().getBytes()));
        KeyFactory keyFactory = KeyFactory.getInstance("RSA");
        return keyFactory.generatePrivate(privKeySpec);
```

```
        }
```

The above code makes a request to get the default password of the instance with the instance id given. It base64 decodes the password string it receives and then RSA decrypts it using the private key file. The getKeyFromFile method reads the key from a file after stripping off the envelope headers and returns the private key. Let's look at the Enable Remote Desktop Tab Page. It's shown below.

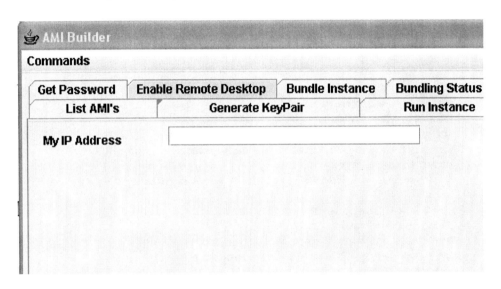

Figure 7 - Enable Remote Desktop Tab Page

```
Enable Remote Desktop event handler code

private class EnableRemoteDesktop extends AbstractAction {

        private EnableRemoteDesktop() {

                // JFormDesigner - Action initialization - DO NOT MODIFY   //GEN-BEGIN:initComponents

                // Generated using JFormDesigner Evaluation license - Aditya Yadav

                putValue(NAME, "Enable Remote Desktop");

                // JFormDesigner - End of action initialization  //GEN-END:initComponents
```

```java
            }


        public void actionPerformed(ActionEvent e) {

            try
        {
                        AmazonEC2Client            ec2            =
AmazonClientFactory.getInstance().getEC2Client();


                        AuthorizeSecurityGroupIngressRequest    request    =    new
AuthorizeSecurityGroupIngressRequest();

    request.setGroupName("default");

    request.setFromPort(0);

    request.setIpProtocol("tcp");

    request.setToPort(65535);

    request.setUserId(AmazonConfig.getInstance().getAccessKey());

    request.setCidrIp(textFieldMyIpAddress.getText() + "/32");


    AuthorizeSecurityGroupIngressResponse            response            =
ec2.authorizeSecurityGroupIngress(request);

    request.setIpProtocol("udp");

    response = ec2.authorizeSecurityGroupIngress(request);

        JOptionPane.showMessageDialog(AMIBuilder.this,"Enable    Remote    Desktop
Completed. ");

        }
        catch (Exception ex)
```

```
                {
                    JOptionPane.showMessageDialog(AMIBuilder.this,"Error Executing Enable Remote Desktop." + ex.getMessage());
                }
            }
        }
```

The above method opens up ports 0-65535 on the running instance for tcp & udp protocol access from the given IP Address. Let's look at the Bundle Instance tab page. It is shown below.

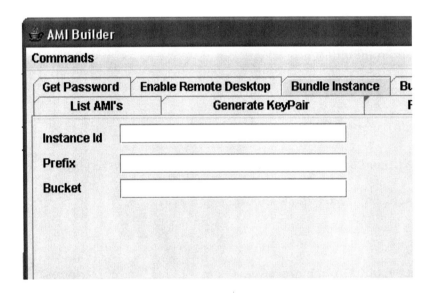

Figure 8 - Bundle Instance Tab Page

Bundle Instance event handler code

```
private class BundleInstance extends AbstractAction {

    private BundleInstance() {

        // JFormDesigner - Action initialization - DO NOT MODIFY   //GEN-BEGIN:initComponents
```

```java
        // Generated using JFormDesigner Evaluation license - Aditya Yadav
        putValue(NAME, "Bundle Instance");
        // JFormDesigner - End of action initialization  //GEN-END:initComponents
    }

    public void actionPerformed(ActionEvent e) {
        try
        {
            AmazonEC2Client ec2 = AmazonClientFactory.getInstance().getEC2Client();

            BundleInstanceRequest request = new BundleInstanceRequest();
            request.setInstanceId(textFieldBundleInstanceInstanceId.getText());
            request.setStorage(new Storage());
            request.getStorage().setS3(new S3Storage());
            request.getStorage().getS3().setAWSAccessKeyId(AmazonConfig.getInstance().getAccessKey());
            request.getStorage().getS3().setBucket(textFieldBundleInstanceBucket.getText());
            request.getStorage().getS3().setPrefix(textFieldBundleInstancePrefix.getText());

            BundleInstanceResponse response = ec2.bundleInstance(request);
            JOptionPane.showMessageDialog(AMIBuilder.this,"Bundle Instance Completed. ");
        }
        catch (Exception ex)
```

```
            {
                JOptionPane.showMessageDialog(AMIBuilder.this,"Error    Executing    Bundle
Instance." + ex.getMessage());
            }
        }
    }
}
```

The above method makes a bundle from the instance with the given instance id and stores in the bucket with the name given. Let's look at Bundle Status Tab Page. Its code is shown below. The tab page has one JTable on it.

Bundle Status event handler code

```
public void actionPerformed(ActionEvent e) {
            try
            {
                    AmazonEC2Client ec2 = AmazonClientFactory.getInstance().getEC2Client();
                    DescribeBundleTasksRequest request = new DescribeBundleTasksRequest();
        DescribeBundleTasksResponse response = ec2.describeBundleTasks(request);
        Object[] columnIdentifiers = new Object[]{"Bundle Id","Bundle State","Error Message","Instance Id"};
            ArrayList data = new ArrayList();
        if (response.getDescribeBundleTasksResult().getBundleTask() != null &&
response.getDescribeBundleTasksResult().getBundleTask().size() != 0)
        {
            for (BundleTask bundleTask :
response.getDescribeBundleTasksResult().getBundleTask())
            {
                if (bundleTask != null)
                {
                    String errorMessage = bundleTask.getBundleTaskError() == null?"":
(bundleTask.getBundleTaskError().getMessage() ==
null?"":bundleTask.getBundleTaskError().getMessage());
                    data.add(new Object[]{bundleTask.getBundleId(),
bundleTask.getBundleState(),errorMessage, bundleTask.getInstanceId()});
                }
            }
        }
            DefaultTableModel tableModel = (DefaultTableModel)tableBundleStatus.getModel();
```

```
            tableModel.setDataVector((Object[][])data.toArray(new Object[0][0]), columnIdentifiers);
            JOptionPane.showMessageDialog(AMIBuilder.this,"Bundle Status Completed. ");
        }
        catch (Exception ex)
        {
            JOptionPane.showMessageDialog(AMIBuilder.this,"Error Executing Bundle Status. " + ex.getMessage());
        }
    }
```

The above method makes a request to get all bundle tasks and updates the JTable on the tab page with the information returned. Let's look at the Register AMI Tab Page as shown below.

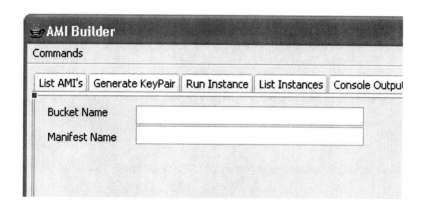

Figure 9 - Register AMI Tab Page

Register AMI event handler code

```
private class RegisterAMI extends AbstractAction {

    private RegisterAMI() {

        // JFormDesigner - Action initialization - DO NOT MODIFY  //GEN-BEGIN:initComponents

        // Generated using JFormDesigner Evaluation license - Aditya Yadav

        putValue(NAME, "Register AMI");

        // JFormDesigner - End of action initialization  //GEN-END:initComponents

    }
```

```java
public void actionPerformed(ActionEvent e) {
    try
    {
        AmazonEC2Client ec2 = AmazonClientFactory.getInstance().getEC2Client();

        RegisterImageRequest request = new RegisterImageRequest();
        request.setImageLocation(textFieldRegisterAMIBucketName.getText() + "/" +textFieldRegisterAMIManifestName.getText());

        RegisterImageResponse response = ec2.registerImage(request);

        JOptionPane.showMessageDialog(AMIBuilder.this,"Register AMI Completed. ");
    }
    catch (Exception ex)
    {
        JOptionPane.showMessageDialog(AMIBuilder.this,"Error Executing Register AMI. " + ex.getMessage());
    }
}
```

The above code registers an ami from the bucket name and the manifest name that you provide. We are all set. Let's build and run the application in the next section.

Using the AMI Builder to Build AMI's

Click Commands->List AMIs the AMI's show up as shown below.

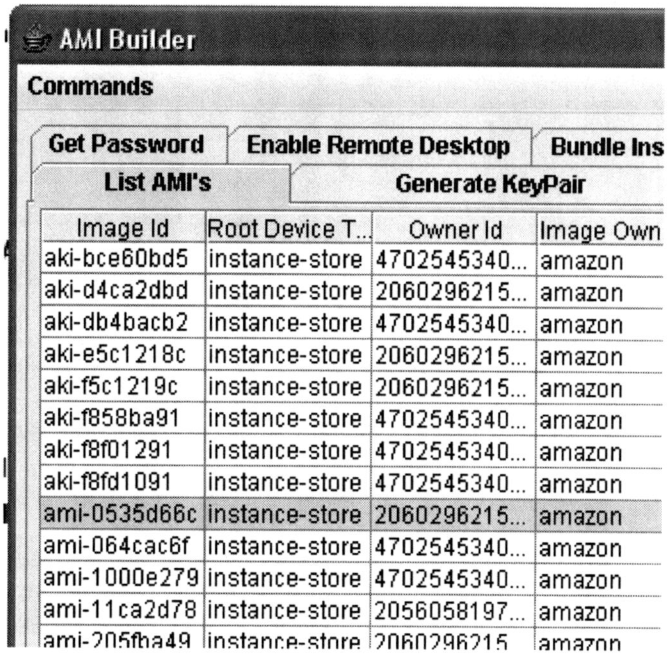

Figure 10 - List AMIs

The ami 'ami-0535d66c' also shows up. This one is the standard Windows 2003 Server image with SQL Server Express installed on it that Amazon provides. We will run an instance of it and bundle it for the purpose of this chapters exercise.

Switch to the Generate KeyPair Tab and enter JavaKeyPair as the key pair name and click Commands->Generate KeyPair. The key pair gets generated and the fingerprint and material shows up on the screen. The .key file with the name JavaKeyPair.key has also gotten generated and is saved in the project folder. We will be using it to access passwords of our running instances in a bit.

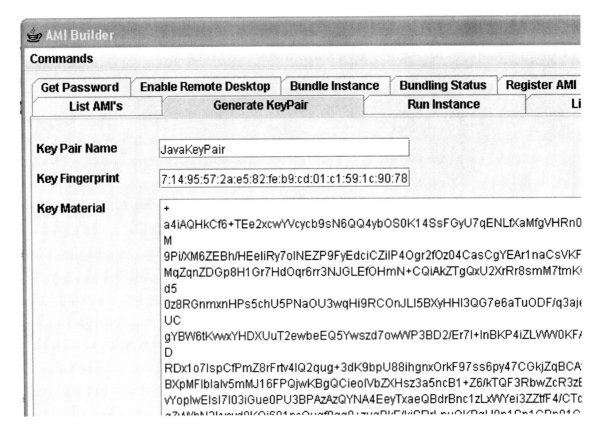

Figure 11 - Generate Key Pair

Switch to the Run Instance Tab and enter the AMI Image Id as 'ami-0535d66c' key pair name as 'JavaKeyPair' and instance type 'm1.large'. Click Commands->Run Instance. AWS will run an instance based on the information given. Click Commands->List Instances every 1 minute for the next 10 odd minutes the instance will show up as running.

Figure 12 - Run Instance

Owner Id	Requester Id	Reservation Id	Image Id	Instance Id	State	Instance Type
572840208927		r-69ed6b01	ami-11ca2d78	i-adebc8c5	terminated	m1.small
572840208927	058890971305	r-89f274e1	ami-0957b260	i-31f7d459	terminated	m1.small
572840208927	058890971305	r-0bf07663	ami-f51aff9c	i-75f5d61d	terminated	m1.small
572840208927	058890971305	r-ddf076b5	ami-ccf615a5	i-edf5d685	terminated	m1.small
572840208927	058890971305	r-5ff17737	ami-1515f67c	i-65f4d70d	terminated	m1.small
572840208927		r-d1f177b9	ami-0535d66c	i-f5f4d79d	running	m1.large

Figure 13 - List Instances

Lets check the Console Output, switch to Console Output Tab and enter the instance id we see in the List Instances tab, click Commands->Console Output. See below.

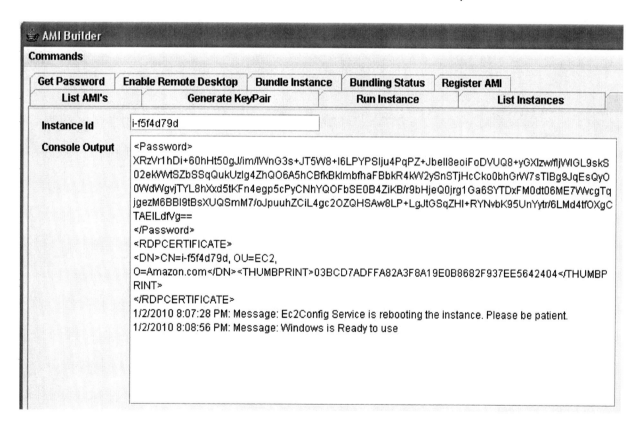

Figure 14 - Console Output

Switch to Get Password Tab enter the instance id and key pair name which is JavaKeyPair in our case, click Commands->Get Password and the administrator password shows up on the screen.

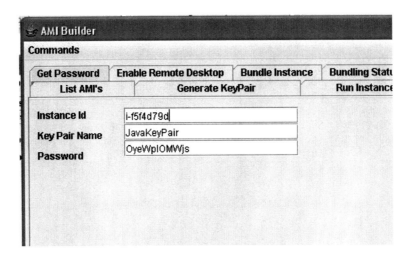

Figure 15 - Get Password

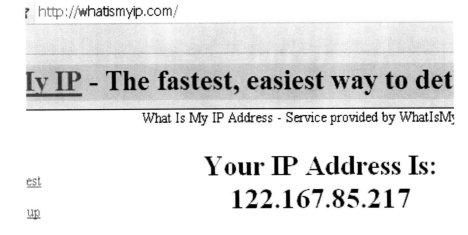

Figure 16 - What is My IP

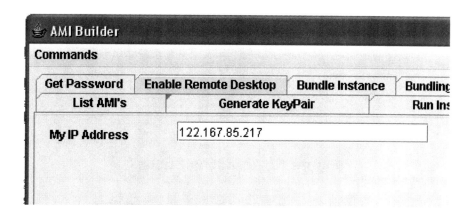

Figure 17 - Enable Remote Desktop

But before that we have to open up the ports. Goto http://whatismyip.com and find out your public ip address, goto Enable Remote Desktop tab and enter your public ip and click Commands->Enable Remote Desktop. Get the public DNS of the instance from list instances tab.

Now you can use Remote Desktop to make any changes to the system, install software etc. After you are done setting up the machine with the software you need. Use the S3Manager software in the source code to create a bucket with a unique name, I will use the name 'javaamibucket'. Back in AMI Builder on the Bundle Instance tab enter the instance id, jav as prefix and 'javaamibucket' as the bucket name. Click Commands->Bundle Instance and click Commands->Bundling Status every minute for about 10-20 minutes. The bundling would complete in 10-20 minutes. It shows up as follows.

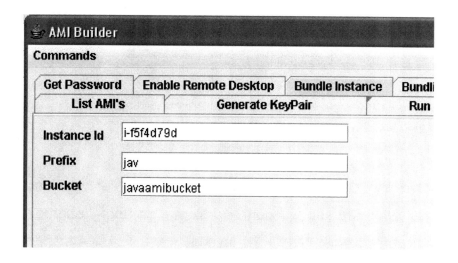

Figure 18 - Bundle Instance

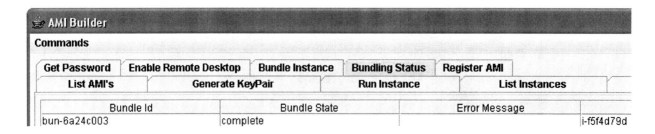

Figure 19 - Bundling Status

Time to register the AMI. Switch to the Register AMI tab and enter javaamibucket as the bucket name and jav.manifest.xml as the manifest name which you can find from the S3Manager by looking at the contents of the 'javaamibucket'. And click Commands-> Register AMI. Click Commands->List AMIs the ami we just made shows up in the list.

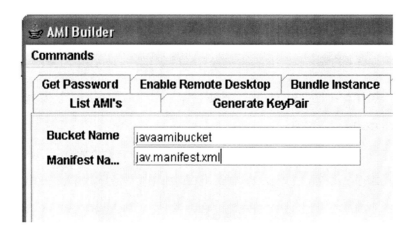

Figure 20 - Register AMI

ami-5048a839	instance-store	4702545340...	amazon	ec2-paid-ibm-images/ib...	machine	Public		i386	
ami-5248a83b	instance-store	4702545340...	amazon	ec2-paid-ibm-images/ib...	machine	Public		i386	
ami-5647a33f	instance-store	2060296215...	amazon	ec2-public-images/fedora...	machine	Public		i386	
ami-5ee70037	instance-store	2056058197...	amazon	/aws-console-quickstart-...	machine	Public		i386	
ami-5efc1137	instance-store	5728402089...		javaamibucket/jav.manife...	machine	Private		windows	x86_64
ami-60da3d09	instance-store	2056058197...	amazon	/aws-console-quickstart-...	machine	Public		i386	
ami-6671910f	instance-store	4702545340...	amazon	ec2-paid-ibm-images/we...	machine	Public		i386	
ami-6776950e	instance-store	4702545340...	amazon	ec2-paid-ibm-images/we...	machine	Public		i386	

Figure 21 - AMI Shows up

Time to terminate and delete everything, Terminate the running instance from the Amazon Console otherwise you will continue to pay an hourly charge, deregister the AMI from the Amazon Console, delete the javamibucket. To understand how to use the Amazon console see the next chapter.

Retrospective

We built our first application in this chapter using the AWS API's. Then we used the application to create a KeyPair, launch runtime instances from available AMI's, access console logs, retrieve admin password, login into the machine, make changes and install software, bundle the instance and then register the bundle as an ami.

Chapter 2- Amazon Management Console

The Amazon management console is the control panel to the Amazon cloud. It provides three consoles, one each for EC2, Elastic MapReduce and CloudFront. We shall go through each one in this chapter.

Amazon EC2

After you login you can select Amazon EC2, the dashboard will load up. See below. In the left hand navigation pane the first item is Region. If you see the options you can choose from US East, US West and EU West. A region is important for many reasons. Distribution across regions gives reliability in case of catastrophes. Also some regulations require that EU data stay only in EU. This is a growing trend amongst most cloud computing vendors. In the dashboard you will also see Service Health and you will get the option to see complete service health details. The yellow triangle in the Service history indicates problems. And when you hover your mouse over it, it will display the details.

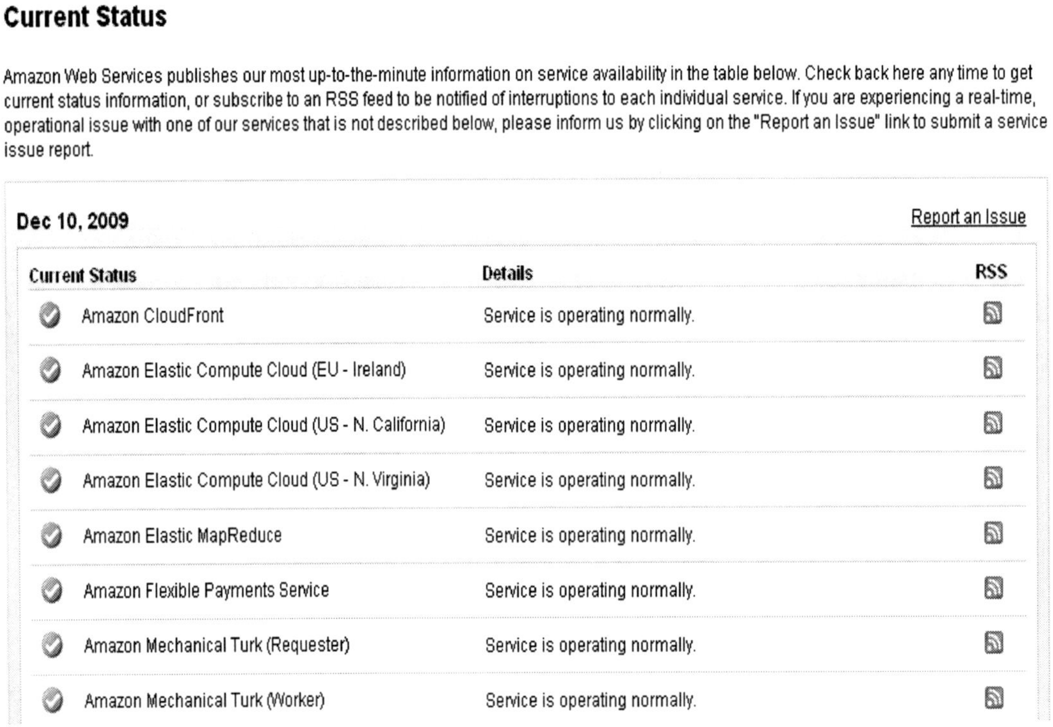

Figure 22 - Service Health

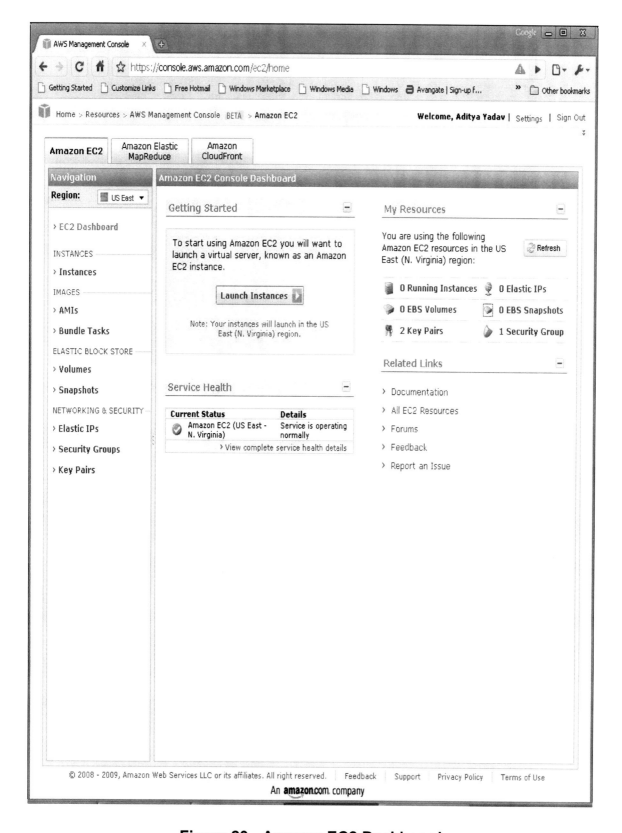

Figure 23 - Amazon EC2 Dashboard

Status History

Amazon Web Services keeps a running log of all service interruptions that we publish in the t the status icons below to see a detailed incident report (click on the icon to persist the popup move forward and backwards through the calendar.

	«	Dec 9	Dec 8	Dec 7
Amazon CloudFront		⊘	⊘	⊘
Amazon EC2 (EU - Ireland)		⊘	⊘	⊘
Amazon EC2 (US - N. California)		⊘	⊘	⊘
Amazon EC2 (US - N. Virginia)		△	⊘	⊘
Amazon Elastic MapReduce		⊘	⊘	⊘
Amazon Flexible Payments Service		⊘	⊘	⊘
Amazon Mechanical Turk (Requester)		△	⊘	⊘
Amazon Mechanical Turk (Worker)		△	⊘	⊘

Figure 24 - Service Status History

The 'my resources' portlet on the right displays resource usage across the cloud. For the financial reports please visit the My Account page. We are not going to cover financials in this chapter. Let's cover a workflow and see what the EC2 Dashboard has to offer us. Let's start with the AMIs item on the Navigation panel. While the dashboard is Ajax intensive it doesn't refresh automatically very often. Every console will have a Refresh button on the right hand top corner. Use it every now and then to see the latest information. You can filter the list of AMIs by using the various filters at the top. One of them is Platform which contains various Linux variants, Open Solaris and Windows. The first filter dropdown lets you filter by EBS instances, instance-store (S3) instances, 32-bit, 64-bit, private, public and Amazon images. We need to find an instance store, windows image to launch. The bottom panel is usually the details panel and displays details of any item selected in the main panel. Enter 0535 in the dynamic filter, the third one on the top. You will see only one AMI. We are going to play around with that.

Figure 25 - Selecting an AMI

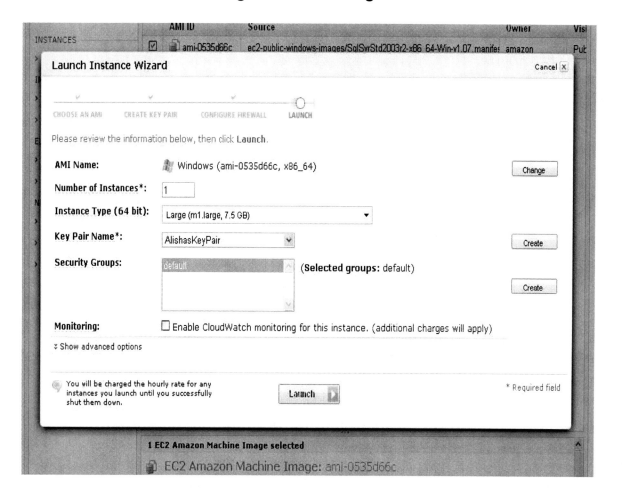

Figure 26 – Launching an Instance

Selecting it enables the Launch button on the top, and also on the context sensitive popup menu. Let's go ahead and launch it. The Launch Instance Wizard pop's up, lets enter 1 instance for now, and I have selected my Key Pair 'AlishasKeyPair'. You would have also created one in the AMI Builder chapter use that one. And leave the default values and click Launch.

Now lets goto the Instances Console. It will show the status as 'starting' it normally takes 5-10 minutes for an instance to launch. So let's check every minute by pressing the Refresh button on the top right. Once is ready it shows up as below. There is also a dropdown at the top of the panel for reserved instances. This has the options of purchasing new reserved instance and viewing reserved instances. Reserved instances are ones you tell Amazon you will need for 1 or 3 years. As of now only Linux/Unix instances are available. The price is calculated per hour of usage for 1 year. Amazon offers a discounted rate. And you can use as much of it as you want. This feature is like taking a season ticket for a Train. You have to pay the amount upfront.

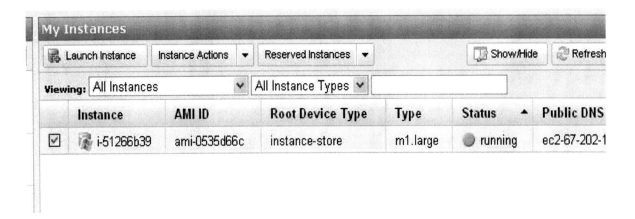

Figure 27 - The Instance Is Running

Our instance is now running. And the instance actions dropdown gets enabled on selecting our instance. It shows the following instance actions as shown in the picture. We will use Get System Log to see the log output from the running instance. Get Windows Admin Password to get the Administrator password. Other options are to Start/Stop/Reboot the instance. Terminate de-provisions it from the cloud. Please note down the Public DNS of the machine, we can use it to gain access to the machine. Let's get the system log.

Figure 28 - Instance Actions

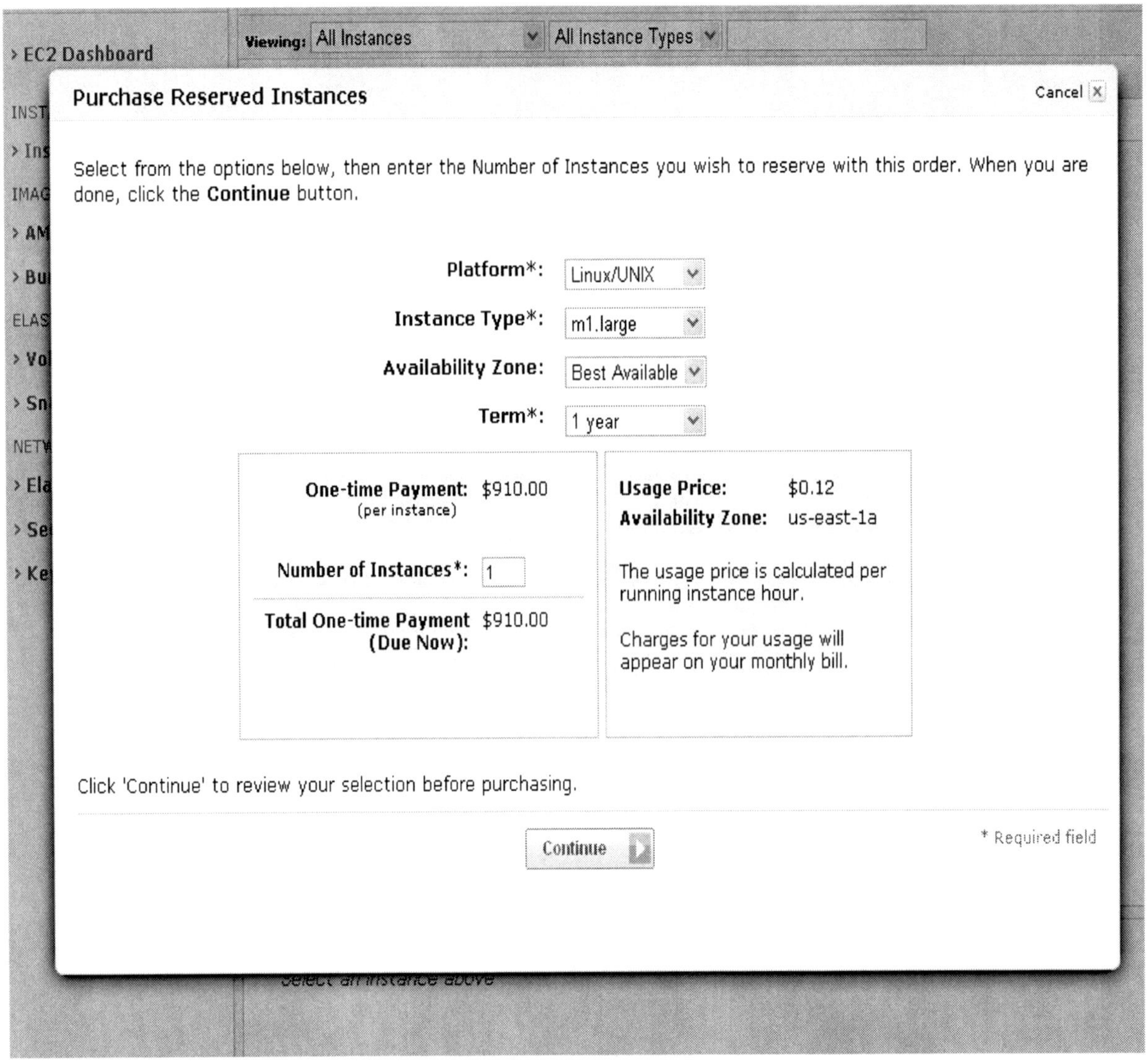

Figure 29 - Purchasing Reserved Instances

Figure 30 - Windows Is Ready To Use

The system log will show "Windows is Ready to use" when the instance is ready to be used.

Let's get the Administrator password. Open the <KeyPairName>.key file from the AMIBuilder folder which we created in the previous chapter. We will need to paste it into the window.

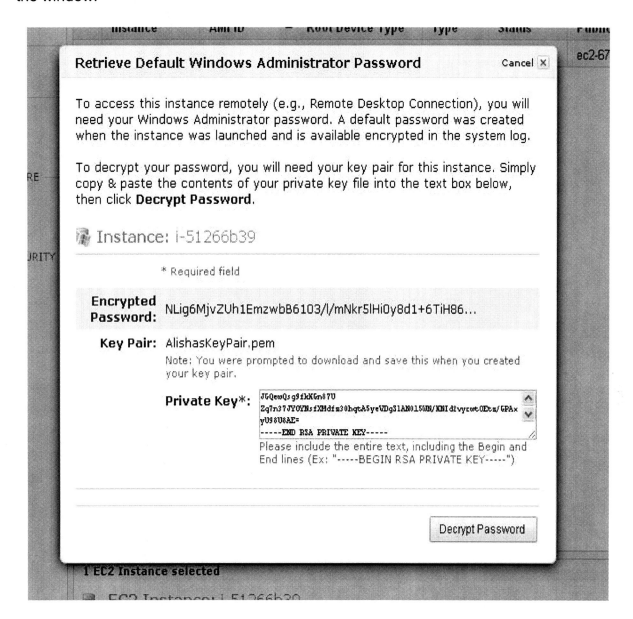

Figure 31 - Retrieving Windows Administrator Password

Click Decrypt Password. And it will show the decrypted password to us. Let's add our Desktop IP address to the Security Group so that we can access the running instance over remote desktop. Click Security Groups Navigation item on the left. We will use the default security group. Select it and goto the details panel at the bottom, resize it a bit. Open http://www.whatismyip.com/ which will display your Desktop's public IP. Create a new entry by selecting RDP and entering <ip>/32 which in my case is 122.15.16.17/32 and click save.

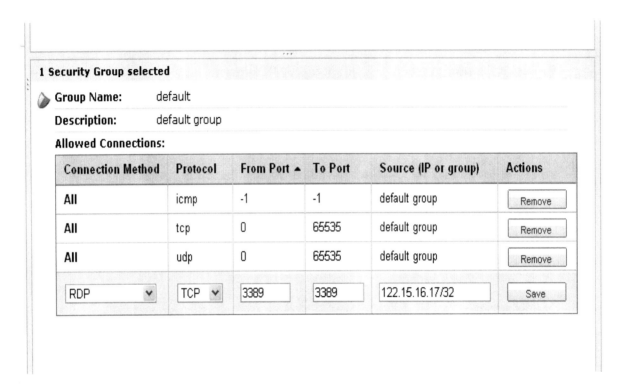

Figure 32 - Adding Your IP to the Default Security Group

Now you can open a Remote Desktop Connection to the running instance using the Public DNS and Administrator Password the login username is Administrator. Go ahead and make whatever changes you would like to.

Next we will create a Bundle from the running instance. Go back to instances panel and select our running instance and choose Bundle Instance (S3 AMI). Enter a unique lowercase bucket name. If it throws an error choose another bucket name that's what I do. I will choose the values 'albuck' (we have created this Bucket using S3 Manager Tool which came along with this book, else an exception will be thrown that the bucket doesn't exist) and 'AlishasKeyPair' and click Bundle. Now goto Bundle Tasks from the navigation pane on the left. Bundling takes between 10-20 minutes. Patience is a virtue.

Refresh Bundle Tasks every 2 minutes. It will display the status as 'complete' when it's done. Time to take a coffee break.

It's done. Selecting the Bundle enables the Button 'Register AMI'. Let's register an AMI from this bundle. You have modified the running instance by installing softwares on it through remote desktop earlier. We will be able to run instances from this image later. Typically we would install our applications on the running instance and create a bundle and register an AMI from it.

Figure 33 - Bundling Complete

Now select the bundle and click Register AMI on it. Now you have your own AMI for use later.

Let's click on Key Pairs from the left navigation pane. Select one. You can see you cannot retrieve your key from here. If you have lost it from your Desktop you will lose access to all the running instances which are using that Key Pair because you will not be able to retrieve Admin passwords for those machines.

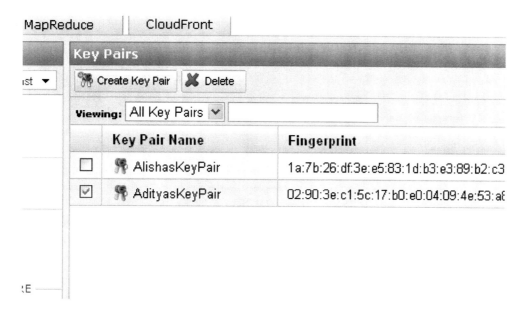

Figure 34 - KeyPairs

Let's create a new Key Pair by clicking the Create Key Pair button on the top. I'm going to name it as MyOtherKeyPair and press create. It will download a file named MyOtherKeyPair.pem to my machine containing the Base64 encrypted RSA Key. I'm going to store it for future use.

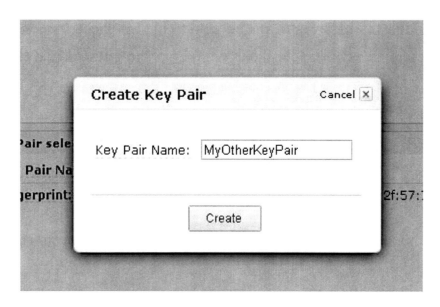

Figure 35 - Creating A KeyPair

Let's go back to AMIs and run an EBS based AMI instance because next we are going to look at the EBS panels. Choose the Filters 'EBS Images', 'Windows' and enter 4808 into the dynamic filter box. And Launch an instance of it. The steps are similar to starting S3 (instance-store) instances.

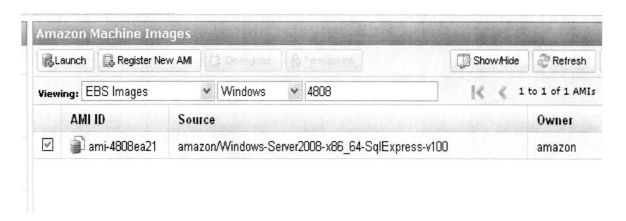

Figure 36 - Running An EBS Based Instance

You can Bundle and Register AMI's of EBS instances similar to S3 instances and we are not going to cover that here.

We have not been enabling CloudWatch Monitoring. It costs a bit but it enables us to gather CPU, Memory and other metrics. Do use it in production environment. For now I'm going to skip it.

Goto Volumes panel. You can filter Volumes by 'Attached Volumes' and 'Detached Volumes' Our EBS volume shows up here. A Volume is like a Hard Disk attached to a Machine (In our case a running instance of a virtual machine)

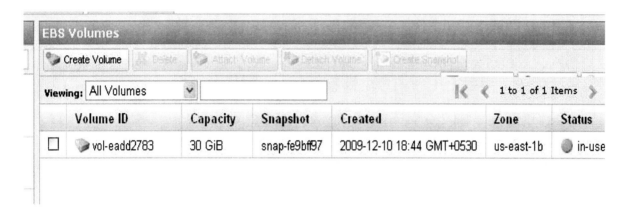

Figure 37 - EBS Volumes Panel

Lets goto Snapshots and take a snapshot of our Volume. Click Create Snapshot button at the top of the panel. Select the Volume and enter a description and hit enter. A Snapshot gets created. It takes a few minutes to do it.

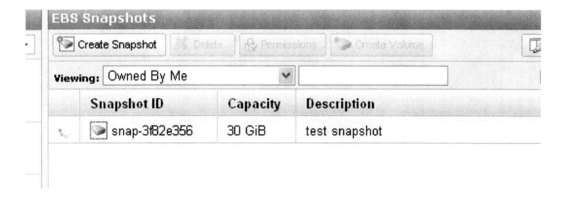

Figure 38 - Creating A Snapshot

Let's get an Elastic IP. And elastic ip is a public internet ip that we can get allocated to ourselves and then point it to any running instance of ours. So if one running instance goes down it doesn't matter we can start another one and if we were using an elastic ip for the previous instance we can point the same elastic ip to the new instance. Goto Elastic IPs panel and click Allocate New Address and confirm in the popup. Let's associate it with one of our instances. Click the Associate button at the top.

Figure 39 - Associate Elastic IP with an Instance

Choose the instance and click associate. You can now hit the IIS server running on the instance through this Elastic IP.

R'ber to de-provision/terminate/delete everything when you are done. To remove the S3 Buckets use the S3 Manager tool provided along with this book.

Amazon Elastic MapReduce

This section is covered in detail in the MapReduce chapter.

Amazon CloudFront

Start the S3 Manager tool provided along with this book (Downloadable from the authors website http://adityayadav.com) and Open the Amazon Console and goto the 'Amazon CloudFront' tab. Before we setup the CloudFront we have to setup a small file object in an S3 bucket.

Enter a unique value for Bucket Name. If the next steps throw errors choose another bucket name. I will choose 'asdfgaditya' Click browse and select some small file. I have chosen a setup log file. Click Put Bucket, you will get a confirmation that it's done. And then click List Buckets. Enter key as 'setup.log' and click Put Object. You will get a confirmation that it's done. Now click List Objects in Bucket. You will be able to see the file object setup.log we just uploaded. Click Make Bucket Public. This will enable CloudFront to serve the Bucket Files.

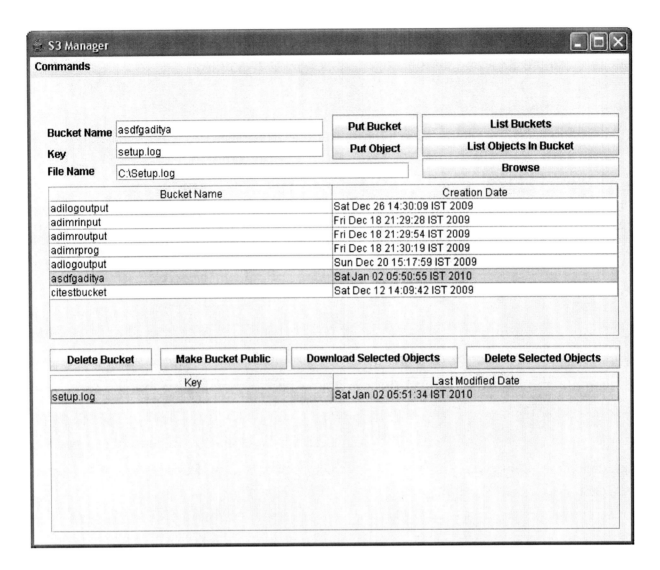

Figure 40 - Public Bucket With 'setup.log'

Now let's look at the Amazon Console, CloudFront tab. Here we can filter by Enabled and Disabled Distributions and also by a dynamic name filter. Lets click Create a Distribution for now. Select 'asdfgaditya' which is the bucket we just created using S3 Manager Tool. And click Create. A CNAME is a custom domain name for your distribution e.g. myimages. It will take a couple of minutes to complete. Keep refreshing every minute using the refresh button on the top right. Selecting the Distribution enables the Enable/Disable, Delete and Edit buttons on the top which are self explanatory.

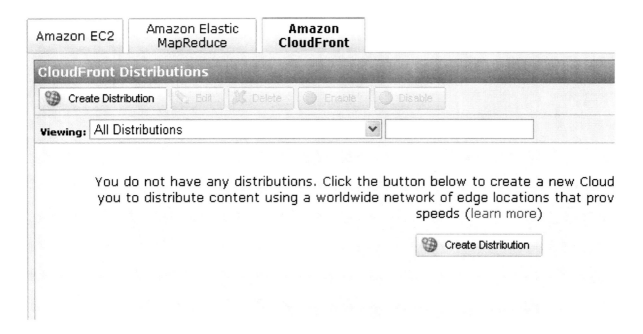

Figure 41 - Amazon CloudFront Console

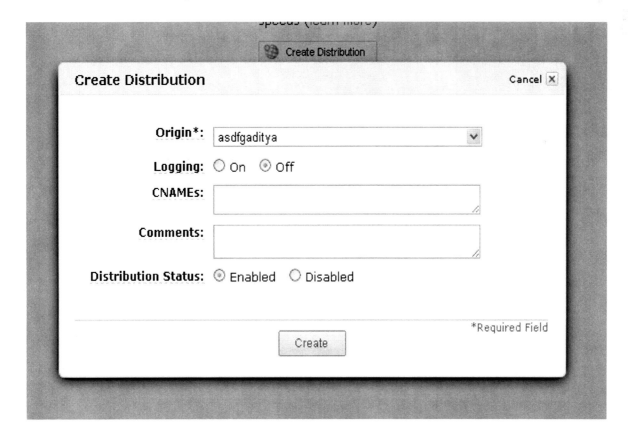

Figure 42 - Creating a Distribution

See the details for the Distribution. You will get the Domain Name from there. See Below.

Domain Name:	d2p9yrpt9bp7r3.cloudfront.net
State:	Deployed
Distribution Status:	● Enabled

Figure 43 - Getting the Domain Name from the Distribution Details

Hit the two urls

1. http://asdfgaditya.s3.amazonaws.com/setup.log

2. http://d2p9yrpt9bp7r3.cloudfront.net/setup.log

Both will download the setup.log file to your desktop. The first one is the direct S3 Bucket URL to the setup.log file. And the second one is being served through the CloudFront Edge servers. Please give 15 minutes for the CloudFront Edge Cache Servers to get updated.

Time to delete everything.

Retrospective

We had a look at the AWS Console. Which had 3 parts one each to manage EC2, MapReduce and CloudFront. We didn't cover MapReduce as it is covered in detail in its own chapter. After this chapter you will be able to manage these three things through the console. Amazon doesn't provide consoles to manage all the functionality and you have to purchase third party tools for them. But as you go through the following chapters you would realize you don't have a need to. As the examples would double as your AWS management application for that particular area/resource.

Chapter 3- Writing our own Monitoring Application

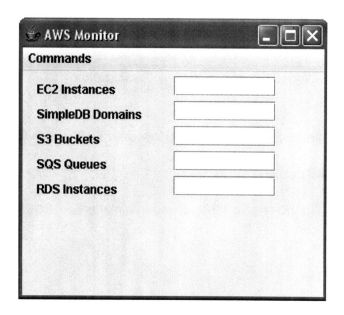

Figure 44 - The Finished Monitoring Application

Every Cloud Deployment needs usage reporting and monitoring. Amazon has not released the API's for reporting so we have to access reports from the My Account section on AWS. We have to monitor our AWS resource usage in every team so that there are no resource leaks. Usually after sometime we forget who owns which instances and whether they were forgotten and left running all this time or they are actually needed. We need monitoring applications, perhaps extensions of this one suited to the purposes of the project. Typically a monitoring application is exposed in full screen mode on a common computer in the team area.

In this chapter we are going to make a tiny monitoring application which is going to show us number of EC2 instances, S3 buckets etc. In a real scenario you will need to create a more elaborate monitoring application and keep it running with a timer so that it refreshes every half an hour or so. The finished AWS Monitor application is shown above. So let's get started.

In the previous chapter we have seen how the AWSManager project is organized and how it contains all the sample applications for most of the chapters.

The refresh event handler

```java
private class RefreshAction extends AbstractAction {

    private RefreshAction() {
        // JFormDesigner - Action initialization - DO NOT MODIFY  //GEN-BEGIN:initComponents
        // Generated using JFormDesigner Evaluation license - Aditya Yadav
        putValue(NAME, "Refresh");
        // JFormDesigner - End of action initialization  //GEN-END:initComponents
    }


    public void actionPerformed(ActionEvent e) {
        updateEC2();
        updateSimpleDB();
        updateS3();
        updateSQS();
        updateRDS();
        JOptionPane.showMessageDialog(AWSMonitor.this, "Update Completed");
    }
}
```

The refresh menu calls various UpdateXXX() methods to update the display with information. Each of the UpdateXXX() methods access the AWS api to collect information and update the respective text boxes. Let's look at the update methods one by one.

updateEC2 method

```java
public void updateEC2(){
    try
    {
        AmazonEC2Client ec2 = AmazonClientFactory.getInstance().getEC2Client();
        DescribeInstancesRequest ec2Request = new DescribeInstancesRequest();
        DescribeInstancesResponse ec2Response = ec2.describeInstances(ec2Request);
        int numInstances = 0;
        numInstances = ec2Response.getDescribeInstancesResult().getReservation().size();
        textFieldEC2Instances.setText(numInstances+"");
    }
    catch (Exception ex)
    {
        JOptionPane.showMessageDialog(this,"Error Refreshing EC2 Information. " + ex.getMessage());
    }
}
```

The above method is responsible for updating the display with EC2 instances count information. It gets the EC2 client from the Amazon Client Factory which is our implementation which takes care of http proxy, amazon authentication etc. and returns clients for various AWS services. The above method makes a describe instances request and counts the number of reservations. Let's look at one more method.

updateRDS

```java
public void updateRDS(){
    try
    {
        AmazonRDSClient rds = AmazonClientFactory.getInstance().getRDSClient();
        DescribeDBInstancesRequest rdsRequest = new DescribeDBInstancesRequest();
        DescribeDBInstancesResponse rdsResponse = rds.describeDBInstances(rdsRequest);
        int numInstances = 0;
        numInstances = rdsResponse.getDescribeDBInstancesResult().getDBInstance().size();
        textFieldRDSInstances.setText(numInstances+"");
    }
    catch (Exception ex)
    {
        JOptionPane.showMessageDialog(this,"Error Refreshing RDS Information. " + ex.getMessage());
    }
}
```

The update RDS method updates the display with number of RDS DB instances. We are going to look at RDS in details in a later chapter. The above code makes a describe DB instances request and counts the number of DB instances and updates the display with the number.

All the other methods are on similar lines. Compile and run the application and click the refresh menu.

Retrospective

We created a tiny monitoring application. Which looks trivial but is very important as in a large team we leak AWS resources, by which we mean that sooner or later you would realize you don't know who owns the resource and whether it was left running and forgotten or is meant to be kept running. AWS Monitor should be extended to monitor the resources and the attributes you are interested in as a team. And it should typically be deployed in full screen mode on a Desktop in the common area which every team member can see.

Chapter 4- Elastic Compute Cloud

According to Amazon "Amazon EC2 is a web service that enables you to launch and manage server instances in Amazon's data centers using APIs or available tools and utilities." You can provision and deprovision servers in the Amazon Data Center at anytime, as many as you want by using the AWS EC2 Console or the EC2 API's. Whether you need 100 servers for 2 days or you need 10,000 for 36 months. The server instances come in various sizes and configurations of Virtual CPU's, RAM and Hard Disks. They are measured in terms of EC2 Compute units for billing purposes. The best part of using Amazon EC2 is that you don't have any upfront capital expenditures to take care of. Companies are still trying to figure out how to operate and manage cloud server instances alongside their in house servers. EC2 is very attractive for occasional e.g. scientific needs or batch processing, or for startups that pay as they go, besides running enterprise applications on them 24x7. EC2 also handles spikes in loads very well with dynamic and auto provisioning of servers. It removes the hassle of managing the datacenter, though servers still need to be administered to a certain extent.

Unlike most packaged offerings EC2 gives you complete access to the infrastructure i.e. you have root access to your machines. You can choose whatever you want to install on them. With EC2 servers at the front and other AWS services like SQS, S3, SimpleDB, and RDS at the back you get an internet scale infrastructure if you would like to. Amazon provides an SLA of 99.95% in every region. The infrastructure is secure and reliable though you still have to take care of compliance requirements in your country/region/industry/domain.

There are two types of instances OnDemand instances and Reserved instances. The former are paid by the hour and involve no commitment on your part. The latter need to be reserved and paid for 1-3 years upfront at a discounted rate. Once reserved you can run the instance at the discounted rate for the rest of the term, if you don't use it there are no usage charges on it.

The various parts of the EC2 offering are as follows-

- Elastic IP addresses
- Elastic Block Store (EBS)
- Virtual Private Cloud
- CloudWatch
- AutoScaling
- Elastic Load Balancing, and
- Multiple Regions

Elastic IP addresses are internet visible IP addresses that you can get allocated to your account and then you can assign them to any running instance. If that instance goes down you can provision another instance with the same image and then reassign the same elastic ip address to the new instance. This will be invisible to the end user except for a small outage.

Elastic Block Store is a persistent storage which can store volumes that can be utilized as the boot partition in server instances or as secondary devices. They can be snapshot'd and restored. EBS is more durable than S3 and volumes get replicated in the background in the same region providing excellent reliability.

Virtual Private Cloud is a mechanism with which you can connect your in house servers with your EC2 instances over a VPN hence forming a Private/Hybrid cloud and to extend your existing management capabilities such as security services, firewalls, and intrusion detection systems to include their AWS resources.

Cloudwatch is a service that allows you to monitor the CPU/ RAM etc. metrics of your instances. There are currently 3 regions US-East, US-West and EU. Separate regions deliver high availability and also cater to e.g. EU requirements of having continent collocated datacenters.

AutoScaling is a mechanism with which server instances can be auto provisioned or deprovisioned based on rules/parameters that you can set. You can use Elastic Load Balancing to automatically distribute incoming application traffic amongst multiple EC2 instances. ELB can detect unhealthy instances and route traffic to healthy ones till the former ones have been restored. Elastic Load Balancing can work with instances in multiple regions providing very high availability and performance. We shall cover each more in their respective chapters.

Retrospective

In this chapter we got a brief overview of EC2. EC2 is at the center of all the Amazon cloud offerings and is covered in other chapters as it pertains to those chapters.

Chapter 5- Cloud Watch

CloudWatch is a simple webservice to provide visibility into the performance and health of your AWS resources. A Measure is an observed value with a name, dimension(s), namespace, unit and timestamp. Measures are the raw data that get aggregated as metrics. A dimension provides further context to a measure e.g. by instanceid, availability zone or autoscaling group. A metric is an aggregation of measures. There are two namespaces in AWS as of now 'AWS/EC2' and 'AWS/ELB' which are data output by EC2 and Elastic Load Balancer respectively. Statistics describe how measure distributions are aggregated e.g. Min, Max, Average, and Sum. Unit is the unit of measurement, every measure has a unit. An example of a measure is 'CPUUtilization' for which Unit is percent and Dimensions are instanceid and instance type [e.g. m1.small, m1.large etc], and the Namespace is 'AWS/EC2'. Other common measures are DiskReadBytes, DiskReadOps, NetworkIn, NetworkOut, DiskWriteBytes, DiskWriteOps etc.

Let's look at the CloudWatch application. It's a small application that uses JFreeChart java library to render the charts. The finished application looks as shown below. It has two tabs, the first one 'Metrics' shows the list of all metrics available for your account. And the second tab will be used to show the chart for a given metric.

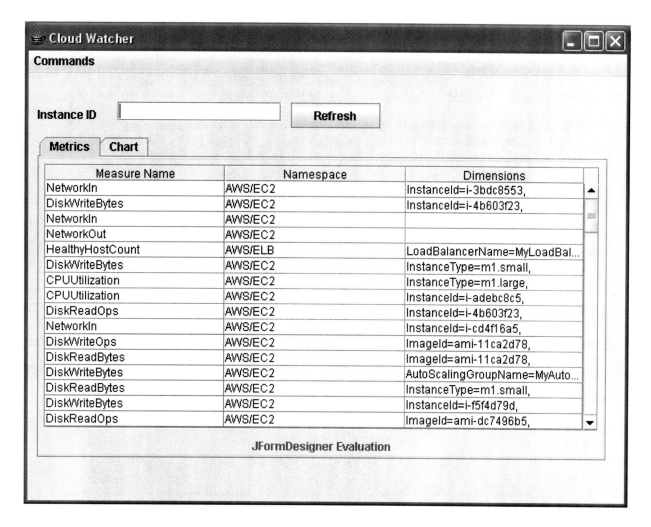

Figure 45 - Finished CloudWatch Application

When the application starts the constructor loads all the metrics available and shows them in the JTable on the first tab. Lets see the constructor code below.

CloudWatch constructor code

```java
public CloudWatch() {
        initComponents();

        this.setDefaultCloseOperation(JFrame.DO_NOTHING_ON_CLOSE);

        try
  {
                AmazonCloudWatchClient cw = AmazonClientFactory.getInstance().getCloudWatchClient();

    ListMetricsRequest request = new ListMetricsRequest();
    ListMetricsResponse response = cw.listMetrics(request);
    Object[] columnIdentifiers = new Object[]{"Measure Name", "Namespace", "Dimensions"};
```

```java
            ArrayList data = new ArrayList();
    for(Metric metric : response.getListMetricsResult().getMetrics())
    {
                    data.add(new Object[]{metric.getMeasureName(),
metric.getNamespace(),new MyDimensions(metric.getDimensions()) });
    }
    DefaultTableModel tableModel = (DefaultTableModel)tableMetrics.getModel();
    tableModel.setDataVector((Object[][])data.toArray(new Object[0][0]), columnIdentifiers);
    JOptionPane.showMessageDialog(CloudWatch.this,"List Metrics Completed. ");
    }
    catch (Exception ex)
    {
        JOptionPane.showMessageDialog(CloudWatch.this,"Error Executing List Metrics. " +
ex.getMessage());
    }
    }
```

The above code is making a ListMetrics request and then it loops over all the metrics returned and extracts Measure Name, Namespace and Dimensions from them and creates one record in the JTable for each metric. It creates a MyDimensions object to hold the Dimenisons list. Let's look at the MyDimensions class below.

MyDimensions class code

```java
class MyDimensions {

        private List<com.amazonaws.cloudwatch.model.Dimension> list = null;

        public MyDimensions(List<com.amazonaws.cloudwatch.model.Dimension> list){
            this.list = list;
        }

        public List<com.amazonaws.cloudwatch.model.Dimension> getList(){
            return list;
        }

        @Override
        public String toString()
    {
        String result = "";
        for (com.amazonaws.cloudwatch.model.Dimension dimension : list)
        {
            result = result + dimension.getName() + "=" + dimension.getValue() + ",";
        }
        return result;
    }
    }
```

This constructor of MyDimensions class takes a Dimension list. It has a method to get the dimension list, and it has a toString() method which converts the dimensions list into a string representation which will have dimension name '=' dimension value separated by comma's. This string will be displayed in the JTable while it will store the original dimensions list which it will use later to query for metrics data.

The application has a refresh button which will refresh the chosen metric for the given instance id. Let's look at the refresh event handler code.

Refresh event handler code

```java
private class Refresh extends AbstractAction {

    private Refresh() {

        // JFormDesigner - Action initialization - DO NOT MODIFY   //GEN-BEGIN:initComponents

        // Generated using JFormDesigner Evaluation license - Aditya Yadav

        putValue(NAME, "Refresh");

        // JFormDesigner - End of action initialization  //GEN-END:initComponents

    }



    public void actionPerformed(ActionEvent e) {

        try {

            String measureName = (String) tableMetrics.getValueAt(tableMetrics.getSelectedRow(),0);

            String nameSpace = (String) tableMetrics.getValueAt(tableMetrics.getSelectedRow(),1);
```

```java
        List<com.amazonaws.cloudwatch.model.Dimension> dimensions = ((MyDimensions) tableMetrics.getValueAt(tableMetrics.getSelectedRow(),2)).getList();

        AmazonCloudWatchClient cw = AmazonClientFactory.getInstance().getCloudWatchClient();


        GetMetricStatisticsRequest request = new GetMetricStatisticsRequest();

        request.setMeasureName(measureName);

        request.setNamespace(nameSpace);

        request.setDimensions(dimensions);

        request.getStatistics().add("Average");

        request.setPeriod(60);

        Date now = new Date();

        java.util.GregorianCalendar gc = new java.util.GregorianCalendar(TimeZone.getTimeZone("GMT"));

        gc.setTime(now);

        now = gc.getTime();

        gc.add(java.util.GregorianCalendar.MINUTE, -30);

        Date startTime = gc.getTime();

        DateFormat format = new SimpleDateFormat("yyyy-MM-dd'T'HH:mm:ss");

        startTime.setMinutes(startTime.getMinutes()+startTime.getTimezoneOffset());

        now.setMinutes(now.getMinutes()+now.getTimezoneOffset());

        request.setStartTime(format.format(startTime));

        request.setEndTime(format.format(now));

        GetMetricStatisticsResponse response = cw.getMetricStatistics(request);
```

```java
        XYSeries series = new XYSeries(measureName);

        int x = 1;

        for(com.amazonaws.cloudwatch.model.Datapoint        point        :
response.getGetMetricStatisticsResult().getDatapoints())

        {

            series.add((float)x, point.getAverage().floatValue());

            x++;

        }

        XYSeriesCollection dataset = new XYSeriesCollection();

        dataset.addSeries(series);


        JFreeChart chart = ChartFactory.createXYLineChart(

            measureName,    // chart title

            "X",            // x axis label

            "Y",            // y axis label

            dataset,        // data

            PlotOrientation.VERTICAL,

            true,           // include legend

            true,           // tooltips

            false           // urls

        );

        final XYPlot plot = chart.getXYPlot();

        final NumberAxis domainAxis = new NumberAxis("x");
```

```
            final NumberAxis rangeAxis = new NumberAxis("y");

            plot.setDomainAxis(domainAxis);

            plot.setRangeAxis(rangeAxis);

            chart.setBackgroundPaint(Color.white);

            plot.setOutlinePaint(Color.black);

            ChartPanel chartPanel = new ChartPanel(chart);

            chartPanel.setPreferredSize(new java.awt.Dimension(500, 270));

            panel2.removeAll();

            panel2.add(chartPanel,BorderLayout.CENTER);

            chartPanel.repaint();

            panel2.repaint();

                        JOptionPane.showMessageDialog(CloudWatch.this,"Refresh Completed. ");

        }

        catch (Exception ex)

        {

            JOptionPane.showMessageDialog(CloudWatch.this,"Error Executing Refresh. " + ex.getMessage());

        }

    }
```

The first thing the above code does is, retrieve the measure name, namespace and dimensions from the selected row in the metrics table. It then makes a request to get metrics statistics, averages for the last half an hour with samples averaged every 60 seconds. It then creates a XYSeries with the datapoints, puts them in a

XYSeriesCollection. It then creates a XYLinechart and puts it on a ChartPanel. Finally it puts the ChartPanel in the Charts Tab. There are some GMT offset calculations so that we get to the UTC time. A Date object is always in local time.

Using CloudWatch

The first thing we have to do is to use AWS Console to launch an instance of an AMI; any AMI would do for the purpose of using cloud watch.

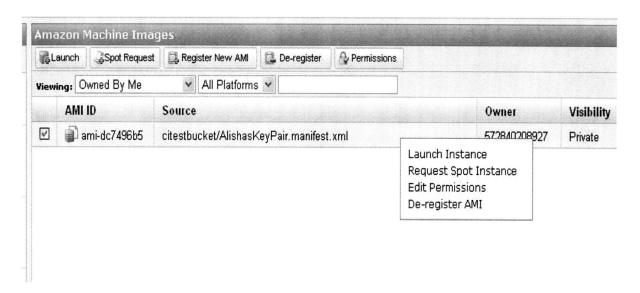

Figure 46 - Launching an Instance

Click continue on the 'Choose An Ami' page.

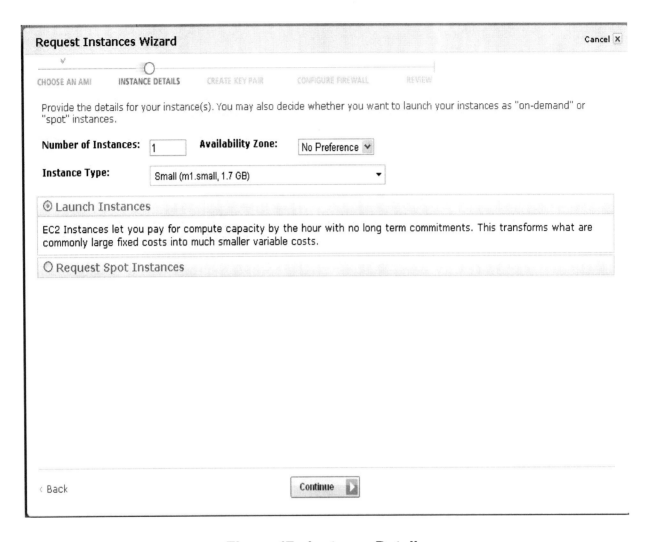

Figure 47 - Instance Details

Enable CloudWatch on the Instance Details page by checking the 'Enable CloudWatch monitoring for this instance' checkbox.

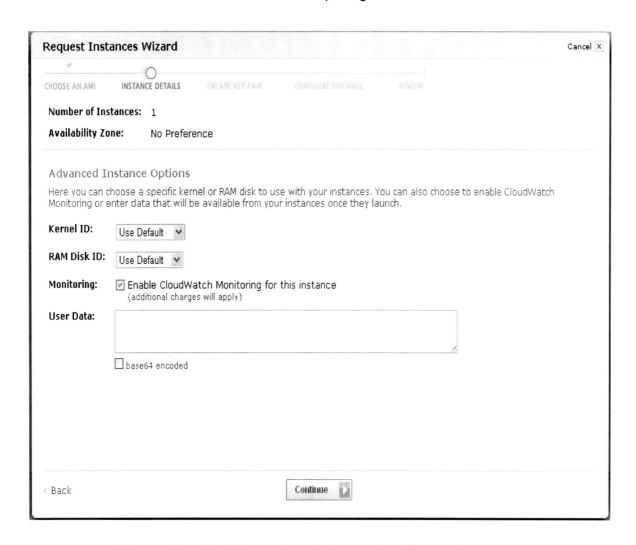

Figure 48 - Enabling Cloud Monitoring For the Instance

Choose the key pair on the Create KeyPair page.

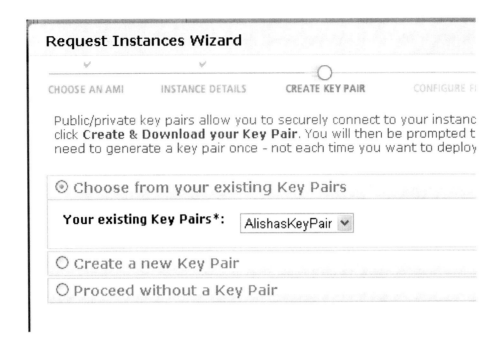

Figure 49 - Associating a KeyPair with the Instance

Configure the firewall on the next page.

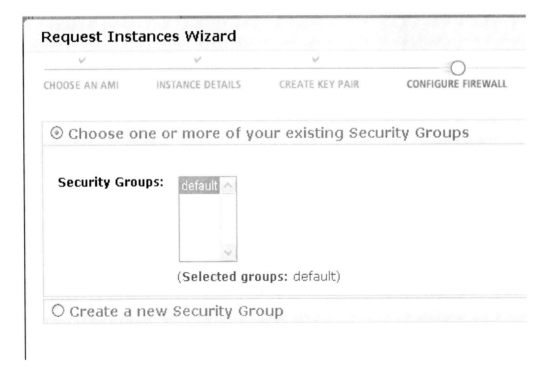

Figure 50 - Configuring Security Groups (FireWall)

Review and launch the instance.

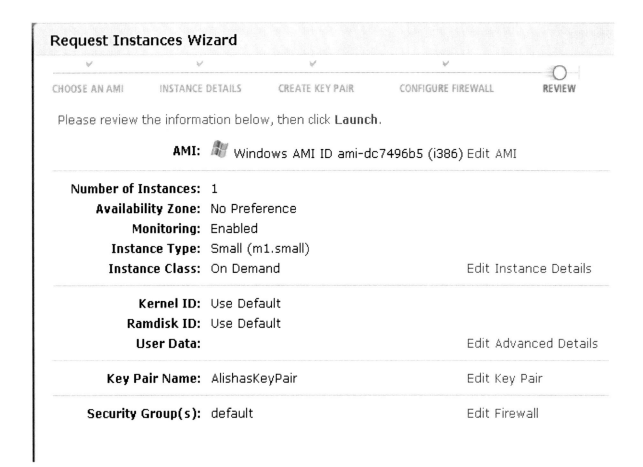

Figure 51 - Reviewing the Instance Configuration before Launching

Now we have to leave the instance running for 15-30 minutes so that the metrics get generated.

Now run the CloudWatch program, it will retrieve the list of metrics and update the list view control. We have to select a measure, lets choose DiskReadBytes, AWS/EC2, InstanceId= i-e7a6858f (you have to choose the one with the instance id of the instance you launched).

Enter the instance id in the text box, click refresh and goto the Chart tab. The chart gets displayed. See below. Refresh the chart after a couple of minutes and the chart will get updated.

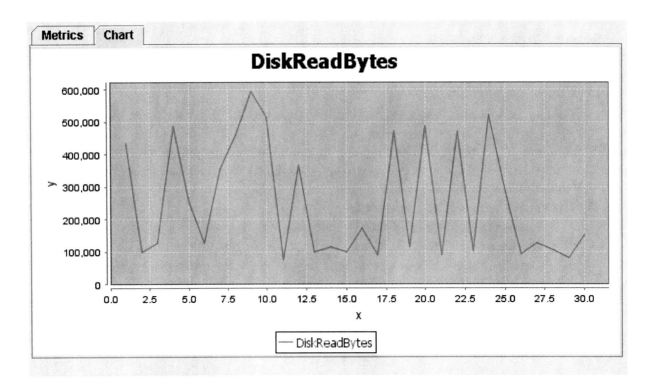

Figure 52 - DiskReadBytes Chart For Instance

Terminate the instance from the AWS Console.

Retrospective

We used CloudWatch to monitor our AWS resources in this chapter for performance. The reader should extend this from one graph at a time application to a multiple simultaneous graphing application and use in a real life scenario to monitor the performance and health of the team's production AWS resources. Typically notifications should be incorporated into the application using messenger, email or sms API's to notify team members when the resource health deteriorates.

Chapter 6- Elastic Load Balancing & Auto Scaling

An Elastic LoadBalancer is a DNS/IP with port(s) which can be accessed by the users of your application. The Elastic LoadBalancer can then spread the load between multiple running instances that you have configured. It can spread loads across multiple availability zones in an EC2 region but not across multiple regions. You can assign any custom domain name to the ELB endpoint so that it appears consistent with the rest of your application resources.

AutoScaling is a way to launch or terminate EC2 Instances depending on a user defined trigger. Which is usually related to some measure on the Elastic LoadBalancer. Instances are created based on preset configurations which you can use to specify the image id, instance type etc. Typically everytime a measure is breached for more than the threshold period one or more new instances are spawned. They will become a part of the configured Elastic LoadBalancer and hence the application will scale up and down depending on the load on the system.

In this chapter we will walkthrough the Elastic LoadBalancer management section in the AWS EC2 console. And we will create an ELB & AS Manager application which we will use to then configure AutoScaling which is not available through the management console.

Start the AWS EC2 Management Console. And launch an instance from the AMI we built, bundled and registered in the Continous Integration chapter, you should finish that chapter and resume at this point. It has Tomcat running our web application and we are going to test that through the Elastic LoadBalancer endpoint.

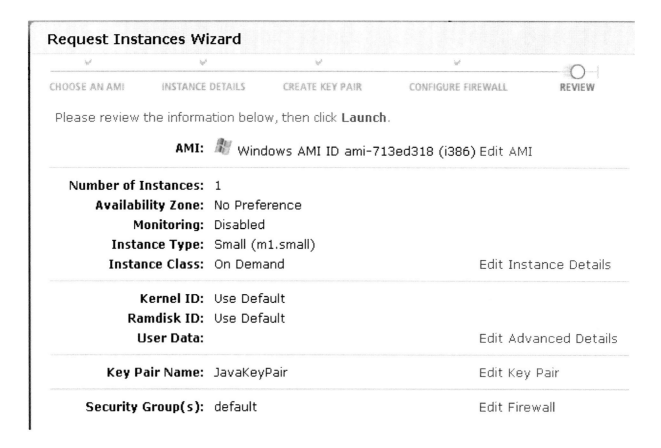

Figure 53 - Launch an Instance from our AMI

Let's wait till the instance is ready.

Figure 54 - Wait Till the Launched Instance Is Running

Go to the LoadBalancers section in the EC2 Console.

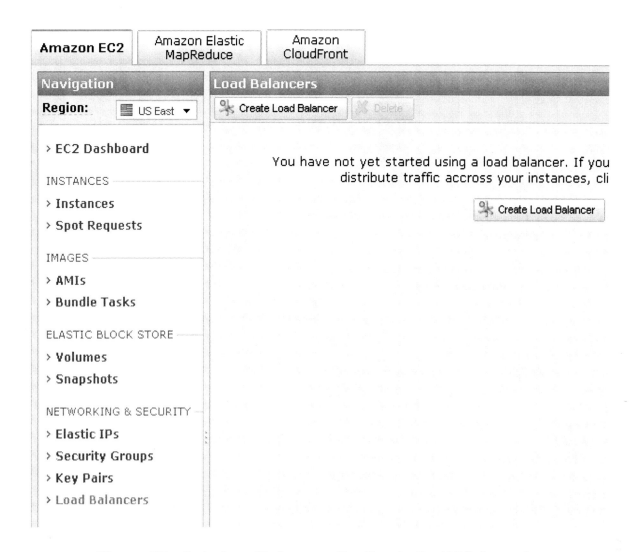

Figure 55 - Goto LoadBalancers Section in the EC2 Console

Let's create a LoadBalancer. Click the 'Create LoadBalancer' button. Remove the first line and create a new one as shown below, which maps incoming connections on port 80 to backend tomcat servers running on port 8080. Click continue on the Define LoadBalancer wizard page.

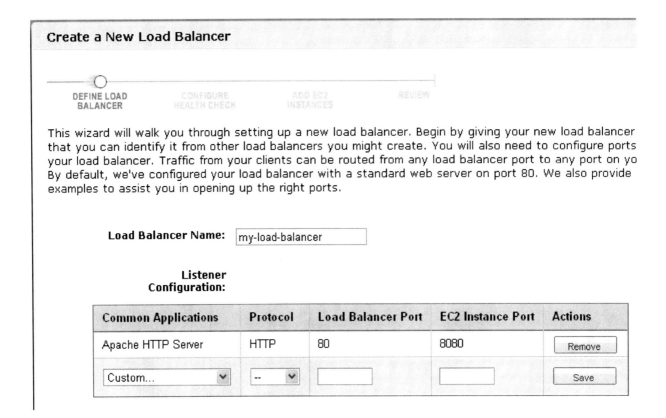

Figure 56 - Define LoadBalancer

We need to configure a way for the LoadBalancer to find out if the instance is healthy or not. We configure '/index.jsp' on our server instances to be hit every 5 minutes. This file is available in the root web application of the Tomcat server and forms a very lightweight mechanism of pinging the server.

We need to enable the LoadBalancer to access the running instances over port 8080 and we should be able to access the load balancer over port 80. For that we have to configure the 'default' security group with Http, 0.0.0.0/0 parameters as shown below.

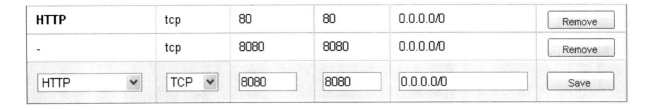

Figure 57 - Enable Instance Access to LoadBalancer and LoadBalancer Access to us

If the page responds in 30 seconds the load balancer will consider the server instance healthy. See Below.

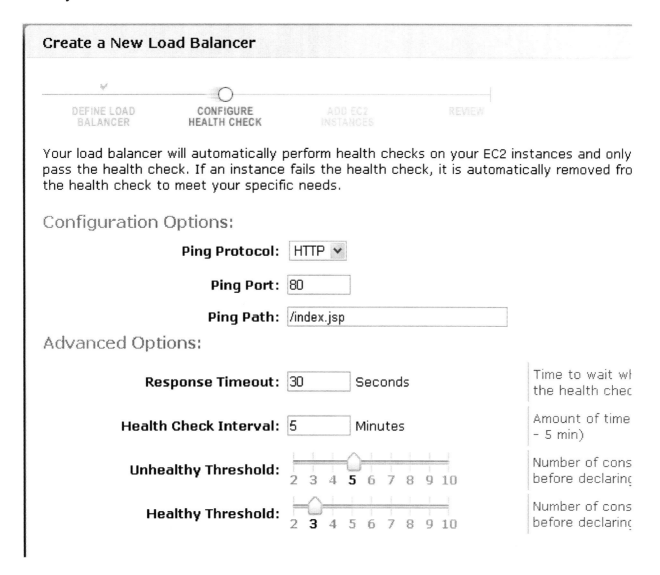

Figure 58 - Configure HealthCheck

Now let's add the instance we launched to the load balancer.

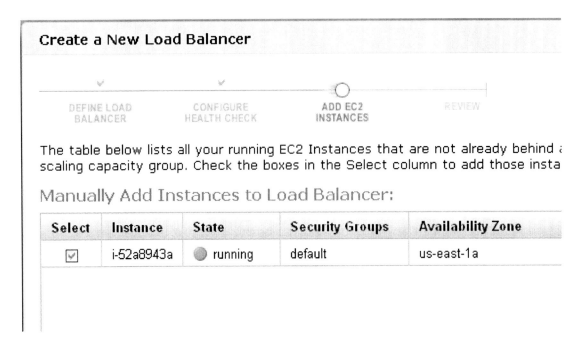

Figure 59 - Add Our Instance to the LoadBalancer

Now Review the configuration and hit Create.

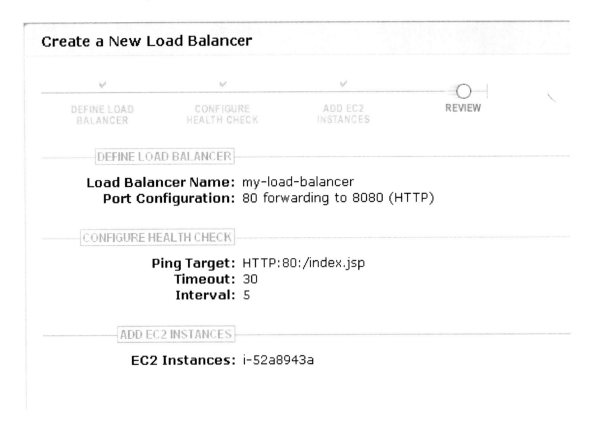

Figure 60 - Review Configuration and Create LoadBalancer

Retrieve the DNS name of the LoadBalancer from the console e.g. my-load-balancer-2040896349.us-east-1.elb.amazonaws.com . The LoadBalancer will take about 10-20 minutes to be ready. Then open a browser and hit http://<LoadBalancerDNS>/AWSToolkitDemo/index.jsp e.g. http://my-load-balancer-2040896349.us-east-1.elb.amazonaws.com/AWSToolkitDemo/index.jsp we will see our login page.

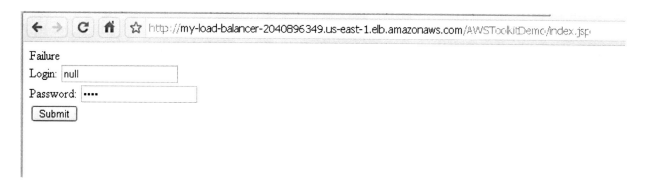

Figure 61 - Website Accessible Through LoadBalancer

Let's create the LoadBalancing and AutoScaling Manager. When finished it looks as shown below.

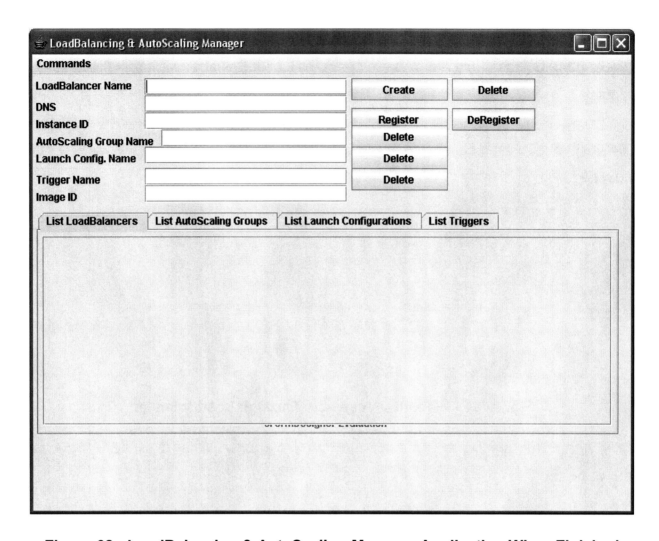

Figure 62 - LoadBalancing & AutoScaling Manager Application When Finished

The menu items are shown below.

Figure 63 - The LoadBalancing AutoScaling Manager Menu

Constructor code

```java
public LoadBalancingAutoScalingManager() {
        initComponents();
        this.setDefaultCloseOperation(JFrame.DO_NOTHING_ON_CLOSE);

        tableListAutoScalingGroups.getSelectionModel().addListSelectionListener(new
ListSelectionListener(){
                public void valueChanged(ListSelectionEvent e) {
                        try {
                                if (!e.getValueIsAdjusting()){
                                        String value = (String)
tableListAutoScalingGroups.getValueAt(tableListAutoScalingGroups.getSelectedRow(),0);
                                        textFieldAutoScalingGroupName.setText(value);
                                }
                        } catch (Exception ex){};
                }
        });
        tableListLaunchConfigurations.getSelectionModel().addListSelectionListener(new
ListSelectionListener(){
                public void valueChanged(ListSelectionEvent e) {
                        try {
                                if (!e.getValueIsAdjusting()){
                                        String value = (String)
tableListLaunchConfigurations.getValueAt(tableListLaunchConfigurations.getSelectedRow(),0);
                                        textFieldLaunchConfig.setText(value);
                                }
                        } catch (Exception ex){};
                }
        });
        tableListLoadBalancers.getSelectionModel().addListSelectionListener(new
ListSelectionListener(){
                public void valueChanged(ListSelectionEvent e) {
                        try {
                                if (!e.getValueIsAdjusting()){
                                        String value = (String)
tableListLoadBalancers.getValueAt(tableListLoadBalancers.getSelectedRow(),0);
                                        textFieldLoadBalancerName.setText(value);
                                }
                        } catch (Exception ex){};
                }
        });
        tableListTriggers.getSelectionModel().addListSelectionListener(new
ListSelectionListener(){
                public void valueChanged(ListSelectionEvent e) {
                        try {
                                if (!e.getValueIsAdjusting()){
                                        String value = (String)
tableListTriggers.getValueAt(tableListTriggers.getSelectedRow(),0);
                                        textFieldTriggerName.setText(value);
                                }
                        } catch (Exception ex){};
                }
```

```
        });
    }
```

The above code sets up selection changed listeners on all the JTables and updates the respective textfields with the names of the items selected in the JTable.

Look at the list loadbalancers event handler code as shown below.

List LoadBalancers event handler code

```
private class ListLoadBalancers extends AbstractAction {

    private ListLoadBalancers() {

        // JFormDesigner - Action initialization - DO NOT MODIFY   //GEN-BEGIN:initComponents

        // Generated using JFormDesigner Evaluation license - Aditya Yadav

        putValue(NAME, "List LoadBalancers");

        // JFormDesigner - End of action initialization  //GEN-END:initComponents

    }


    public void actionPerformed(ActionEvent e) {

        try {

            AmazonElasticLoadBalancingClient elb = AmazonClientFactory.getInstance().getElasticLoadBalancingClient();


            DescribeLoadBalancersRequest request = new DescribeLoadBalancersRequest();

            DescribeLoadBalancersResponse response = elb.describeLoadBalancers(request);

            Object[] columnIdentifiers = new Object[] { "Name",
```

```java
                    "DNS", "Created Time", "Instances"};

            ArrayList data = new ArrayList();
            for (LoadBalancerDescription description : response.getDescribeLoadBalancersResult().getLoadBalancerDescriptions()) {
                data.add(new Object[] { description.getLoadBalancerName(),
                    (description.getDNSName()==null?"":description.getDNSName()),
                    description.getCreatedTime(),
                    ConcatenateInstances(description.getInstances()) });
            }
            DefaultTableModel tableModel = (DefaultTableModel) tableListLoadBalancers.getModel();
            tableModel.setDataVector((Object[][]) data.toArray(new Object[0][0]), columnIdentifiers);

            JOptionPane.showMessageDialog(LoadBalancingAutoScalingManager.this, "List LoadBalancers Completed. ");
        } catch (Exception ex) {
            JOptionPane.showMessageDialog(LoadBalancingAutoScalingManager.this, "Error Executing List LoadBalancers. " + ex.getMessage());
        }
    }

    private String
```

```
ConcatenateInstances(List<com.amazonaws.elasticloadbalancing.model.Instance> list)
    {
        String result = "";
        for (com.amazonaws.elasticloadbalancing.model.Instance instance : list)
        {
            result = result + instance.getInstanceId() + ",";
        }
        return result;
    }
}
```

It makes a request to describe loadbalancers and then iterates over the results to display name, dns, created time and the list of instances the loadbalancer is associated with. The ConcatenateInstances method loops over the instances and adds the names to a string that is displayed in the list view. Look at the Create LoadBalancer event handler code below.

Create LoadBalancer event handler code

```
private class CreateLoadBalancer extends AbstractAction {

    private CreateLoadBalancer() {

        // JFormDesigner - Action initialization - DO NOT MODIFY   //GEN-BEGIN:initComponents

        // Generated using JFormDesigner Evaluation license - Aditya Yadav

        putValue(NAME, "Create");

        // JFormDesigner - End of action initialization   //GEN-END:initComponents
```

```java
        }

        public void actionPerformed(ActionEvent e) {
            try {
                AmazonElasticLoadBalancingClient elb = AmazonClientFactory.getInstance().getElasticLoadBalancingClient();

                CreateLoadBalancerRequest request = new CreateLoadBalancerRequest();

                request.setLoadBalancerName(textFieldLoadBalancerName.getText());

                request.getAvailabilityZones().add("us-east-1a");

                Listener listener = new Listener();

                listener.setInstancePort(8080);

                listener.setLoadBalancerPort(80);

                listener.setProtocol("HTTP");

                request.getListeners().add(listener);

                CreateLoadBalancerResponse response = elb.createLoadBalancer(request);


                ConfigureHealthCheckRequest chcRequest = new ConfigureHealthCheckRequest();

                chcRequest.setLoadBalancerName(textFieldLoadBalancerName.getText());

                HealthCheck healthCheck = new HealthCheck();

                healthCheck.setHealthyThreshold(2);

                healthCheck.setUnhealthyThreshold(2);

                healthCheck.setTimeout(30);
```

```
            healthCheck.setTarget("HTTP:80/index.jsp");

            healthCheck.setInterval(300);

            chcRequest.setHealthCheck(healthCheck);

            ConfigureHealthCheckResponse          chcResponse          =
elb.configureHealthCheck(chcRequest);


            JOptionPane.showMessageDialog(LoadBalancingAutoScalingManager.this,   "Create
LoadBalancer Completed. ");

                } catch (Exception ex) {


            JOptionPane.showMessageDialog(LoadBalancingAutoScalingManager.this,    "Error
Executing Create LoadBalancer." + ex.getMessage());

                }

            }

        }
```

This method does a couple of things. It creates a load balancer in the us east 1a zone with the given name. And creates a HTTP listener that reads on port 80 and forwards to port 8080 on the backend instance. It also configures healthcheck for the load balancer which checks the backend instances every 300 seconds, it hits the page '/index,jsp' on port 8080 on the backend server. This page is installed in the root web application in a standard tomcat installation. This is a mechanism to ping the server. If the server responds to this request within a timeout of 30 seconds 2 consecutive times it is healthy. If it fails 2 consecutive times it is deemed unhealthy and requests are not sent to it anymore. Look at the delete loadbalancer event handler code shown below.

Delete LoadBalancer event handler code

```
private class DeleteLoadBalancer extends AbstractAction {
```

```java
        private DeleteLoadBalancer() {
                // JFormDesigner - Action initialization - DO NOT MODIFY  //GEN-BEGIN:initComponents
                // Generated using JFormDesigner Evaluation license - Aditya Yadav
                putValue(NAME, "Delete");
                // JFormDesigner - End of action initialization  //GEN-END:initComponents
        }


        public void actionPerformed(ActionEvent e) {
            try {
                    AmazonElasticLoadBalancingClient elb = AmazonClientFactory.getInstance().getElasticLoadBalancingClient();


                    DeleteLoadBalancerRequest request = new DeleteLoadBalancerRequest();
                request.setLoadBalancerName(textFieldLoadBalancerName.getText());

                DeleteLoadBalancerResponse response = elb.deleteLoadBalancer(request);


            JOptionPane.showMessageDialog(LoadBalancingAutoScalingManager.this, "Delete LoadBalancer Completed. ");

                } catch (Exception ex) {


            JOptionPane.showMessageDialog(LoadBalancingAutoScalingManager.this, "Error Executing Delete LoadBalancer." + ex.getMessage());
                }
        }
```

```
        }
```

This method makes a request to delete the loadbalancer with the given name. Look at the Register Instance with LoadBalancer event handler code shown below.

Register Instance with LoadBalancer event handler code

```java
private class Register extends AbstractAction {

    private Register() {

        // JFormDesigner - Action initialization - DO NOT MODIFY   //GEN-BEGIN:initComponents
        // Generated using JFormDesigner Evaluation license - Aditya Yadav
        putValue(NAME, "Register");
        // JFormDesigner - End of action initialization  //GEN-END:initComponents

    }


    public void actionPerformed(ActionEvent e) {

        try {

            AmazonElasticLoadBalancingClient elb = AmazonClientFactory.getInstance().getElasticLoadBalancingClient();

            RegisterInstancesWithLoadBalancerRequest request = new RegisterInstancesWithLoadBalancerRequest();

            request.setLoadBalancerName(textFieldLoadBalancerName.getText());

            Instance instance = new Instance();

            instance.setInstanceId(textFieldInstanceID.getText());
```

```
            request.getInstances().add(instance);

        RegisterInstancesWithLoadBalancerResponse         response         =
elb.registerInstancesWithLoadBalancer(request);


        JOptionPane.showMessageDialog(LoadBalancingAutoScalingManager.this,    "Register
Instance With LoadBalancer Completed. ");

            } catch (Exception ex) {


        JOptionPane.showMessageDialog(LoadBalancingAutoScalingManager.this,    "Error
Executing Register Instance With LoadBalancer." + ex.getMessage());

            }
        }
    }
```

The above method makes a request to register an instance with the given instance id with the loadbalancer. Once registered the load balancer will start passing requests to the instance. Look at the following code to DeRegister the Instance with the LoadBalancer.

DeRegister Instance With LoadBalancer event handler code

```
private class DeRegister extends AbstractAction {

        private DeRegister() {

            // JFormDesigner - Action initialization - DO NOT MODIFY  //GEN-BEGIN:initComponents

            // Generated using JFormDesigner Evaluation license - Aditya Yadav

            putValue(NAME, "DeRegister");

            // JFormDesigner - End of action initialization  //GEN-END:initComponents
```

```java
        }


        public void actionPerformed(ActionEvent e) {

            try {

                AmazonElasticLoadBalancingClient elb = AmazonClientFactory.getInstance().getElasticLoadBalancingClient();


                DeregisterInstancesFromLoadBalancerRequest request = new DeregisterInstancesFromLoadBalancerRequest();

                request.setLoadBalancerName(textFieldLoadBalancerName.getText());

                Instance instance = new Instance();

                instance.setInstanceId(textFieldInstanceID.getText());

                request.getInstances().add(instance);

                DeregisterInstancesFromLoadBalancerResponse response = elb.deregisterInstancesFromLoadBalancer(request);


                JOptionPane.showMessageDialog(LoadBalancingAutoScalingManager.this, "DeRegister Instance With LoadBalancer Completed. ");

            } catch (Exception ex) {

                JOptionPane.showMessageDialog(LoadBalancingAutoScalingManager.this, "Error Executing DeRegister Instance With LoadBalancer." + ex.getMessage());

            }
        }
    }
```

The above method deregisters the instance with the given instance id from the loadbalancer. Look at the event handler to list autoscaling groups shown below.

List AutoScaling Groups event handler code

```
private class ListautoScalingGroups extends AbstractAction {

    private ListautoScalingGroups() {

        // JFormDesigner - Action initialization - DO NOT MODIFY   //GEN-BEGIN:initComponents

        // Generated using JFormDesigner Evaluation license - Aditya Yadav

        putValue(NAME, "List AutoScaling Groups");

        // JFormDesigner - End of action initialization  //GEN-END:initComponents

    }


    public void actionPerformed(ActionEvent e) {
        try {

            AmazonAutoScalingClient asc = AmazonClientFactory.getInstance().getAutoScalingClient();


            DescribeAutoScalingGroupsRequest request = new DescribeAutoScalingGroupsRequest();

            DescribeAutoScalingGroupsResponse response = asc.describeAutoScalingGroups(request);

            Object[] columnIdentifiers = new Object[] { "Name", "Created Time", "Launch Config Name","LoadBalancers","Min Size","Max Size"};
```

```java
        ArrayList data = new ArrayList();
        for (AutoScalingGroup group : response.getDescribeAutoScalingGroupsResult().getAutoScalingGroups()) {
            data.add(new Object[] { group.getAutoScalingGroupName(),
                    group.getCreatedTime().toString(),
                    group.getLaunchConfigurationName(),
                    ConcatenateLoadBalancerNames(group.getLoadBalancerNames()),
                    group.getMinSize()+"",
                    group.getMaxSize()+""});
        }
        DefaultTableModel tableModel = (DefaultTableModel) tableListAutoScalingGroups.getModel();
        tableModel.setDataVector((Object[][]) data.toArray(new Object[0][0]), columnIdentifiers);

        JOptionPane.showMessageDialog(LoadBalancingAutoScalingManager.this, "List AutoScaling Groups Completed. ");
        } catch (Exception ex) {

            JOptionPane.showMessageDialog(LoadBalancingAutoScalingManager.this, "Error Executing List AutoScaling Groups. " + ex.getMessage());
        }
    }
    private String ConcatenateLoadBalancerNames(List<String> list)
    {
```

```
        String result = "";
    for (String name : list)
    {
       result = result + name + ",";
    }
    return result;
  }
      }
```

The above code updates the JTable for showing AutoScaling Groups. It uses a utility method to concatenate the associated loadbalancer names into a string. Look at the list launch configurations event handler code shown below.

List Launch Configurations event handler code

```
private class ListLaunchConfigurations extends AbstractAction {
        private ListLaunchConfigurations() {
                // JFormDesigner - Action initialization - DO NOT MODIFY   //GEN-BEGIN:initComponents
                // Generated using JFormDesigner Evaluation license - Aditya Yadav
                putValue(NAME, "List Launch Configurations");
                // JFormDesigner - End of action initialization  //GEN-END:initComponents
        }


        public void actionPerformed(ActionEvent e) {
                try {
```

```java
AmazonAutoScalingClient asc = AmazonClientFactory.getInstance().getAutoScalingClient();

DescribeLaunchConfigurationsRequest request = new DescribeLaunchConfigurationsRequest();
DescribeLaunchConfigurationsResponse response = asc.describeLaunchConfigurations(request);
Object[] columnIdentifiers = new Object[] { "Name", "Created Time", "Key Name","Instance Type","Image ID"};

ArrayList data = new ArrayList();
for (LaunchConfiguration config : response.getDescribeLaunchConfigurationsResult().getLaunchConfigurations()) {
    data.add(new Object[] { config.getLaunchConfigurationName(),
        config.getCreatedTime().toString(),
        config.getKeyName(),
        config.getInstanceType(),
        config.getImageId()});
}
DefaultTableModel tableModel = (DefaultTableModel) tableListLaunchConfigurations.getModel();
tableModel.setDataVector((Object[][]) data.toArray(new Object[0][0]), columnIdentifiers);

JOptionPane.showMessageDialog(LoadBalancingAutoScalingManager.this, "List Launch
```

```
Configurations Completed. ");
                } catch (Exception ex) {

            JOptionPane.showMessageDialog(LoadBalancingAutoScalingManager.this,    "Error Executing List Launch Configurations. " + ex.getMessage());
                }
            }
        }
```

The above method updates the JTables with the launch configurations details. Look at the List Triggers event handler code shown below.

List Triggers event handler code

```
private class ListTriggers extends AbstractAction {

        private ListTriggers() {

            // JFormDesigner - Action initialization - DO NOT MODIFY    //GEN-BEGIN:initComponents

            // Generated using JFormDesigner Evaluation license - Aditya Yadav

            putValue(NAME, "List Triggers");

            // JFormDesigner - End of action initialization  //GEN-END:initComponents
        }


        public void actionPerformed(ActionEvent e) {

            try {

                AmazonAutoScalingClient    asc    = AmazonClientFactory.getInstance().getAutoScalingClient();
```

```java
DescribeTriggersRequest request = new DescribeTriggersRequest();

request.setAutoScalingGroupName(textFieldAutoScalingGroupName.getText());

DescribeTriggersResponse response = asc.describeTriggers(request);

Object[] columnIdentifiers = new Object[] { "Name",

"Created Time", "Measure Name","Namespace","Period","Lower Threshold","Lower Breach Incr.","Upper Threshold",

"Upper Breach Incr.", "Breach Duration"};


ArrayList data = new ArrayList();

for (Trigger trigger : response.getDescribeTriggersResult().getTriggers()) {

    data.add(new Object[] { trigger.getTriggerName(),

        trigger.getCreatedTime().toString(),

        trigger.getMeasureName(),

        trigger.getNamespace(),

        trigger.getPeriod()+"",

        trigger.getLowerThreshold()+"",

        trigger.getLowerBreachScaleIncrement(),

        trigger.getUpperThreshold()+"",

        trigger.getUpperBreachScaleIncrement(),

        trigger.getBreachDuration()});

}

DefaultTableModel tableModel = (DefaultTableModel)
```

```
            tableListTriggers.getModel();

                         tableModel.setDataVector((Object[][]) data.toArray(new Object[0][0]), columnIdentifiers);


        JOptionPane.showMessageDialog(LoadBalancingAutoScalingManager.this, "List Triggers Completed. ");

                 } catch (Exception ex) {


        JOptionPane.showMessageDialog(LoadBalancingAutoScalingManager.this, "Error Executing List Triggers. " + ex.getMessage());

                     }

                 }

             }
```

The above method updates the JTable with the detail of Trigger's. Look at the Delete AutoScaling Group event handler code shown below.

Delete AutoScaling Group event handler code

```
private class DeleteAutoScalingGroup extends AbstractAction {

        private DeleteAutoScalingGroup() {

             // JFormDesigner - Action initialization - DO NOT MODIFY  //GEN-BEGIN:initComponents

             // Generated using JFormDesigner Evaluation license - Aditya Yadav

             putValue(NAME, "Delete");

             // JFormDesigner - End of action initialization  //GEN-END:initComponents

        }
```

```java
public void actionPerformed(ActionEvent e) {
    try {
        AmazonAutoScalingClient asc = AmazonClientFactory.getInstance().getAutoScalingClient();

        DescribeAutoScalingGroupsRequest asgRequest = new DescribeAutoScalingGroupsRequest();

        asgRequest.getAutoScalingGroupNames().add(textFieldAutoScalingGroupName.getText());

        DescribeAutoScalingGroupsResponse asgResponse = asc.describeAutoScalingGroups(asgRequest);


        for (com.amazonaws.autoscaling.model.Instance instance : asgResponse.getDescribeAutoScalingGroupsResult().getAutoScalingGroups().get(0).getInstances())
        {
            String instanceId = instance.getInstanceId();

            TerminateInstanceInAutoScalingGroupRequest tiasgRequest = new TerminateInstanceInAutoScalingGroupRequest();

            tiasgRequest.setInstanceId(instanceId);

            asc.terminateInstanceInAutoScalingGroup(tiasgRequest);
        }

        DeleteAutoScalingGroupRequest request = new DeleteAutoScalingGroupRequest();

        request.setAutoScalingGroupName(textFieldAutoScalingGroupName.getText());
```

```
            DeleteAutoScalingGroupResponse response = asc.deleteAutoScalingGroup(request);

        JOptionPane.showMessageDialog(LoadBalancingAutoScalingManager.this,    "Delete AutoScaling Group Completed. ");
            } catch (Exception ex) {

        JOptionPane.showMessageDialog(LoadBalancingAutoScalingManager.this,    "Error Executing Delete AutoScaling Group." + ex.getMessage());
            }
        }
    }
```

This method iterates over all the running instances in the AutoScaling Group and terminates them. It then deletes the AutoScaling Group. Look at the Delete LaunchConfig event handler code shown below.

Delete LaunchConfig event handler code

```
private class DeleteLaunchConfig extends AbstractAction {
    private DeleteLaunchConfig() {
        // JFormDesigner - Action initialization - DO NOT MODIFY   //GEN-BEGIN:initComponents
        // Generated using JFormDesigner Evaluation license - Aditya Yadav
        putValue(NAME, "Delete");
        // JFormDesigner - End of action initialization  //GEN-END:initComponents
    }
```

```java
public void actionPerformed(ActionEvent e) {
    try {
        AmazonAutoScalingClient asc = AmazonClientFactory.getInstance().getAutoScalingClient();

        DeleteLaunchConfigurationRequest request = new DeleteLaunchConfigurationRequest();

        request.setLaunchConfigurationName(textFieldLaunchConfig.getText());

        DeleteLaunchConfigurationResponse response = asc.deleteLaunchConfiguration(request);

        JOptionPane.showMessageDialog(LoadBalancingAutoScalingManager.this, "Delete Launch Config Completed. ");
    } catch (Exception ex) {

        JOptionPane.showMessageDialog(LoadBalancingAutoScalingManager.this, "Error Executing Delete Launch Config." + ex.getMessage());
    }
}
```

The above method deletes the Launch Configuration with the given name. Look at the Delete Trigger event handler code shown below.

Delete Trigger event handler code

```java
private class DeleteTrigger extends AbstractAction {

    private DeleteTrigger() {
```

```java
        // JFormDesigner - Action initialization - DO NOT MODIFY  //GEN-BEGIN:initComponents
        // Generated using JFormDesigner Evaluation license - Aditya Yadav
        putValue(NAME, "Delete");
        // JFormDesigner - End of action initialization  //GEN-END:initComponents
    }


    public void actionPerformed(ActionEvent e) {
        try {
            AmazonAutoScalingClient asc = AmazonClientFactory.getInstance().getAutoScalingClient();

            DeleteTriggerRequest request = new DeleteTriggerRequest();
            request.setTriggerName(textFieldTriggerName.getText());
            request.setAutoScalingGroupName(textFieldAutoScalingGroupName.getText());
            DeleteTriggerResponse response = asc.deleteTrigger(request);

            JOptionPane.showMessageDialog(LoadBalancingAutoScalingManager.this, "Delete Trigger Completed. ");
        } catch (Exception ex) {
            JOptionPane.showMessageDialog(LoadBalancingAutoScalingManager.this, "Error Executing Delete Trigger." + ex.getMessage());
        }
    }
}
```

```
        }
```

This method deletes the Trigger with the given name and belonging to the given AutoScaling Group name. Look at the 'Create AutoScaled LoadBalancer' event handler code shown below.

Create AutoScaled LoadBalancer event handler code

```
private class CreateAutoScaledLoadBalancer extends AbstractAction {

        private CreateAutoScaledLoadBalancer() {

                // JFormDesigner - Action initialization - DO NOT MODIFY   //GEN-BEGIN:initComponents

                // Generated using JFormDesigner Evaluation license - Aditya Yadav

                putValue(NAME, "Create AutoScaled LoadBalancer");

                // JFormDesigner - End of action initialization  //GEN-END:initComponents

        }


        public void actionPerformed(ActionEvent e) {

                try {

                        AmazonAutoScalingClient asc = AmazonClientFactory.getInstance().getAutoScalingClient();

                        AmazonElasticLoadBalancingClient elb = AmazonClientFactory.getInstance().getElasticLoadBalancingClient();


                        CreateLoadBalancerRequest clbRequest = new CreateLoadBalancerRequest();

                        clbRequest.setLoadBalancerName(textFieldLoadBalancerName.getText());
```

```java
Listener listener = new Listener();

listener.setInstancePort(8080);

listener.setLoadBalancerPort(80);

listener.setProtocol("HTTP");

clbRequest.getListeners().add(listener);

clbRequest.setLoadBalancerName(textFieldLoadBalancerName.getText());

clbRequest.getAvailabilityZones().add("us-east-1a");

CreateLoadBalancerResponse clbResponse = elb.createLoadBalancer(clbRequest);


// configure the healthcheck

ConfigureHealthCheckRequest chcRequest = new ConfigureHealthCheckRequest();

chcRequest.setLoadBalancerName(textFieldLoadBalancerName.getText());

HealthCheck healthCheck= new HealthCheck();

healthCheck.setHealthyThreshold(2);

healthCheck.setUnhealthyThreshold(2);

healthCheck.setTimeout(30);

healthCheck.setTarget("HTTP:80/index.jsp");

healthCheck.setInterval(300);

chcRequest.setHealthCheck(healthCheck);

ConfigureHealthCheckResponse chcResponse = elb.configureHealthCheck(chcRequest);



// create the launch configuration
```

```java
CreateLaunchConfigurationRequest clcRequest = new CreateLaunchConfigurationRequest();

    clcRequest.setInstanceType("m1.small");

    clcRequest.setLaunchConfigurationName(textFieldLaunchConfig.getText());

    clcRequest.setImageId(textFieldImageID.getText());

    CreateLaunchConfigurationResponse clcResponse = asc.createLaunchConfiguration(clcRequest);


    //Create autoscaling group

    CreateAutoScalingGroupRequest casgRequest = new CreateAutoScalingGroupRequest();

    casgRequest.getAvailabilityZones().add("us-east-1a");

    casgRequest.setAutoScalingGroupName(textFieldAutoScalingGroupName.getText());

    casgRequest.setLaunchConfigurationName(textFieldLaunchConfig.getText());

    casgRequest.getLoadBalancerNames().add(textFieldLoadBalancerName.getText());

    casgRequest.setMinSize(1);

    casgRequest.setMaxSize(3);

    CreateAutoScalingGroupResponse casgResponse = asc.createAutoScalingGroup(casgRequest);


    CreateOrUpdateScalingTriggerRequest coustRequest = new CreateOrUpdateScalingTriggerRequest();

    coustRequest.setAutoScalingGroupName(textFieldAutoScalingGroupName.getText());

    com.amazonaws.autoscaling.model.Dimension dimension = new com.amazonaws.autoscaling.model.Dimension();
```

```java
            dimension.setName("AutoScalingGroupName");

            dimension.setValue(textFieldAutoScalingGroupName.getText());

            coustRequest.getDimensions().add(dimension);

            coustRequest.setMeasureName("CPUUtilization");

            coustRequest.setStatistic("Average");

            coustRequest.setTriggerName(textFieldTriggerName.getText());

            coustRequest.setNamespace("AWS/EC2");

            coustRequest.setPeriod(60);

            coustRequest.setLowerThreshold(40);

            coustRequest.setLowerBreachScaleIncrement("-1");

            coustRequest.setUpperThreshold(80);

            coustRequest.setUpperBreachScaleIncrement("1");

            coustRequest.setBreachDuration(600);

            CreateOrUpdateScalingTriggerResponse coustResponse = asc.createOrUpdateScalingTrigger(coustRequest);

            JOptionPane.showMessageDialog(LoadBalancingAutoScalingManager.this, "Create AutoScaled LoadBalancer Completed. ");

        } catch (Exception ex) {

            JOptionPane.showMessageDialog(LoadBalancingAutoScalingManager.this, "Error Executing Create AutoScaled LoadBalancer." + ex.getMessage());

        }
    }
}
```

This method is the main method in the Manager. It does a couple of things to setup an AutoScaled LoadBalancing configuration. It creates a loadbalancer with a HTTP protocol port 80 to port 8080 forwarding listener. Configures a health check. Creates a launch configuration with the given AMI Image Id. Creates an AutoScaling Group with minimum size 1 and maximum size 3. And Creates a CPUUtilization trigger with 40-80% thresholds. To increase the instance's if 80% is breached for more than 5 minutes and to decrease the instance's if it dips below 40%.

Using LoadBalancing & AutoScaling Manager

Start the Manager and enter 'MyLoadBalancer' as the LoadBalancer name, click Create, and click Commands->List LoadBalancers. The LoadBalancer gets created and showsup in the LoadBalancers list view. But it doesn't have any instances. See Below.

Figure 64 - Create LoadBalancer through the Manager

We have an instance running from the previous exercise which was based on an AMI we bundled and registered earlier. Let's provide the instance id and register that instance, by clicking the Register button, with this LoadBalancer. Then click Commands-> List LoadBalancers and the instance shows up associated with the LoadBalancer, as shown below.

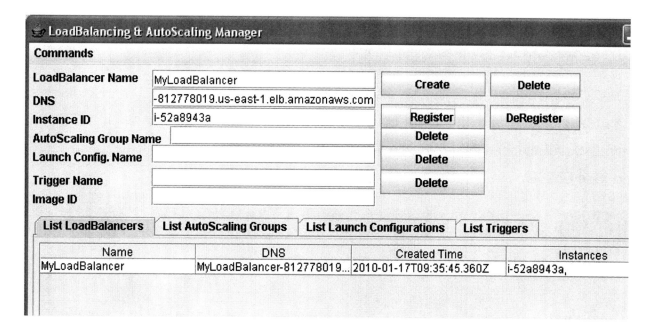

Figure 65 - Register Instance with the LoadBalancer Using the Manager

We have already added HTTP, 0.0.0.0/0 to the default security group earlier for ports 80 & 8080, which is required to allow the LoadBalancer access to the Tomcat on port 8080 on the running instances, and also for us to access the load balancer. If you have skipped the previous exercise create the entries in the 'default' security group for the same using the AWS Management Console.

Wait for 10-20 minutes for the LoadBalancer to get ready and then open the browser and hit 'http://<LoadBalancerDNS>/AWSToolkitDemo/index.jsp' the login page loads up. We are all set.

Now De-Register the instance from the LoadBalancer by clicking the De-Register button, click Delete button next to the LoadBalancer Name to delete the LoadBalancer, click Commands->List LoadBalancers. An empty list shows up. Also terminate the running instance from the AWS EC2 Management Console.

Now let's setup an AutoScaled configuration. Enter MyLoadBalancer as the LoadBalancer Name, MyautoScalingGroup as the AutoScaling Group Name, MyLaunchConfig as the Launch Config. Name and MyTrigger as the Trigger Name, in

Image Id text box enter the AMI Image Id of the bundle we created and registered as AMI earlier, which has our website on it.

Click Commands->Create AutoScaled LoadBalancer and then Click Commands->List LoadBalancers. Copy the DNS of the LoadBalancer. Wait for 20 minutes and hit http://<LoadBalancerDNS>/AWSToolkitDemo/index.jsp. Our website login page loads up. See Below.

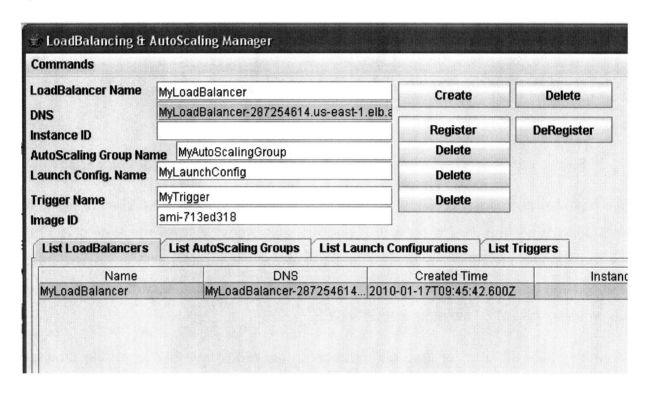

Figure 66 - Create AutoScaled LoadBalancer Using Manager

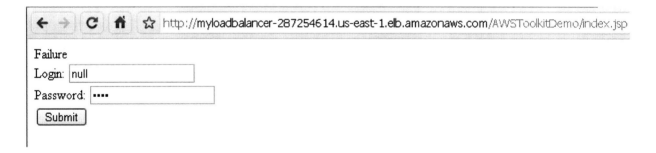

Figure 67 - Website Accessible Through LoadBalancer

Now delete the LoadBalancer, AutoScaling Group, Launch Config and the Trigger.

Retrospective

We created a LoadBalancer using the AWS EC2 Management Console. And we did the same through the Manager which we developed. We also create an AutoScaled LoadBalanced Configuration using the Manager. We did all the heavylifting through one Create AutoScaled LoadBalancer method. There is a lot of scope to improve the manager to make it flexible enough to handle various use cases. It is left to the user to modify the Manager to suite his project needs.

Chapter 7- Simple Storage Service

Simple Storage Service or S3 allows you to store data in the cloud and to upload and download the data from anywhere on the world wide internet. A Bucket is a container used to store data in S3. All bucket names must be globally unique. As they are mapped to a subdomain through which you can download the data/files. You can store an unlimited number of objects in a bucket, with the limit of 5GB per object. You can control permissions on your buckets and objects. Each object is identified by a key which is unique in that bucket. An S3 bucket can implement a virtual filesystem using paths as keys.

Every bucket can be accessed through an internet URL like http://<bucketname>.s2.amazonaws.com. Every bucket can have objects stored in them which are identified by keys and can have a tag associated with them, they can be downloaded from http://<bucket>.s3.amazonaws.com/<objectkey>. Simple Storage Service or S3 can also form the backend for CloudFront which can then distribute the objects through global edge servers. S3 is also used to store AMI's in Amazon, MapReduce Input/Output/Programs & Logs, and our application data.

In this chapter we will create an Amazon S3 Manager which will help us manage buckets and objects. See the picture below to see what the manager looks like when complete.

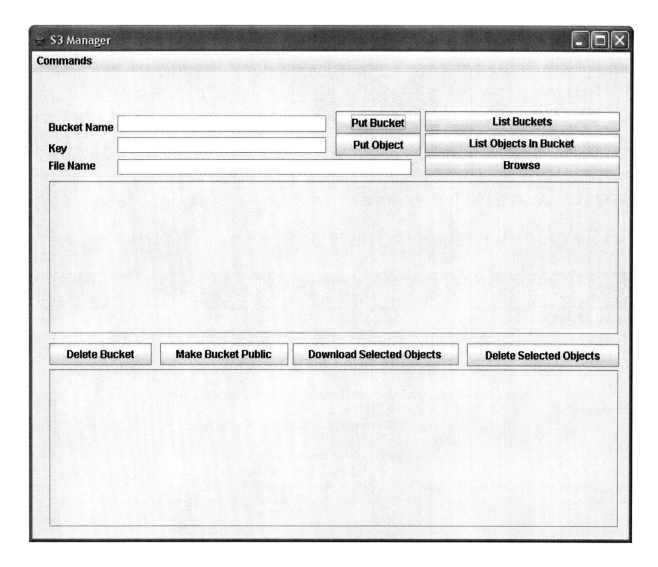

Figure 68 - The Finished S3 Manager Application

Let's see what the application does. It uses your Amazon secret keys and the java wrapper for Amazon S3 API's to communicate to Amazon Web Services. If you enter a bucket name and press Put Bucket it will create a bucket for you. And it will respond with a confirmation. If an error is returned means the name is not appropriate or it is not globally unique, choose a different name. Click List Buckets to see the list of your buckets. Browse for a file (a small one for now) and enter <filename> as the key and press Put Object. It will create an object in the selected bucket for you. Click List Objects in Bucket to see all the objects in the selected bucket.

If you select a bucket from the bucket list it will update the Bucket Name text box. So that other commands can work on that bucket. The bottom list view is for objects and has multiple selections enabled. Selecting an object in the objects list will populate the Key textbox. Delete Selected Objects deletes the selected objects in the list view in the current bucket. Delete Bucket deletes the current bucket if it's empty. Download Selected Objects will prompt you to select a folder and will download all the selected objects into that folder as files with the key(s) as the filename(s).

Let's see some code to make all this happen. The constructor has the following code.

Constructor

```java
public S3Manager() {
        initComponents();

        this.setDefaultCloseOperation(JFrame.DO_NOTHING_ON_CLOSE);

        tableS3BucketList.getSelectionModel().addListSelectionListener(new ListSelectionListener(){
                public void valueChanged(ListSelectionEvent e) {
                        try {
                                if (!e.getValueIsAdjusting()){
                                        String value = (String) tableS3BucketList.getValueAt(tableS3BucketList.getSelectedRow(),0);
                                        textFieldBucketName.setText(value);
                                }
                        } catch (Exception ex){};
                }
        });

        tableS3ObjectsList.getSelectionModel().addListSelectionListener(new ListSelectionListener(){
                public void valueChanged(ListSelectionEvent e) {
                        try {
                                if (!e.getValueIsAdjusting()){
                                        String value = (String) tableS3ObjectsList.getValueAt(tableS3ObjectsList.getSelectedRow(),0);
                                        textFieldKey.setText(value);
                                }
                        } catch (Exception ex){};
                }
        });
}
```

The constructor contains code to update the bucket name and key text boxes when the selection in the buckets jtable and the objects jtable changes. Let's see the code for the Put Bucket button.

Put Bucket event handler code

```java
private class PutBucket extends AbstractAction {

    private PutBucket() {
        // JFormDesigner - Action initialization - DO NOT MODIFY     //GEN-BEGIN:initComponents
        // Generated using JFormDesigner Evaluation license - Aditya Yadav
        putValue(NAME, "Put Bucket");
        // JFormDesigner - End of action initialization  //GEN-END:initComponents
    }


    public void actionPerformed(ActionEvent e) {
        try
        {
            S3Service s3 = AmazonClientFactory.getInstance().getS3Service();
            s3.createBucket(textFieldBucketName.getText());
            JOptionPane.showMessageDialog(S3Manager.this,"Put Bucket Completed. ");
        }
        catch (Exception ex)
        {
            JOptionPane.showMessageDialog(S3Manager.this,"Error Executing Put Bucket. " + ex.getMessage());
```

```
            }
        }
    }
```

The code makes a simple create bucket request with the bucket name desired. Let's see the code for Put Object button.

Put Object event handler

```
private class PutObject extends AbstractAction {
            private PutObject() {
                        // JFormDesigner - Action initialization - DO NOT MODIFY  //GEN-BEGIN:initComponents
                        // Generated using JFormDesigner Evaluation license - Aditya Yadav
                        putValue(NAME, "Put Object");
                        // JFormDesigner - End of action initialization  //GEN-END:initComponents
            }

            public void actionPerformed(ActionEvent e) {
                    try
            {
                            S3Service s3 = AmazonClientFactory.getInstance().getS3Service();
                            S3Object s3Object = new S3Object(new File(textFieldFileName.getText()));
                            s3Object.setKey(textFieldKey.getText());
                    s3.putObject(textFieldBucketName.getText(),s3Object);
                    JOptionPane.showMessageDialog(S3Manager.this,"Put Object Completed. ");
            }
            catch (Exception ex)
            {
                    JOptionPane.showMessageDialog(S3Manager.this,"Error Executing Put Object. " + ex.getMessage());
            }
            }
        }
```

Put Object makes a request with the bucket name, key and the file object for the file you want to upload as object. It then displays a success message and returns.

Let's see the List Buckets button method.

List Buckets event handler code

```java
private class ListBuckets extends AbstractAction {

    private ListBuckets() {

        // JFormDesigner - Action initialization - DO NOT MODIFY  //GEN-BEGIN:initComponents

        // Generated using JFormDesigner Evaluation license - Aditya Yadav

        putValue(NAME, "List Buckets");

        // JFormDesigner - End of action initialization  //GEN-END:initComponents

    }


    public void actionPerformed(ActionEvent e) {

        try
        {

            S3Service s3 = AmazonClientFactory.getInstance().getS3Service();

            S3Bucket[] buckets = s3.listAllBuckets();

            Object[] columnIdentifiers = new Object[]{"Bucket Name", "Creation Date"};

            ArrayList data = new ArrayList();


            for (int i=0; i<buckets.length; i++){

                data.add(new Object[]{buckets[i].getName(), buckets[i].getCreationDate().toString()});

            }

            DefaultTableModel tableModel = (DefaultTableModel)tableS3BucketList.getModel();

            tableModel.setDataVector((Object[][])data.toArray(new Object[0][0]),
```

```
columnIdentifiers);
                        JOptionPane.showMessageDialog(S3Manager.this,"List    Buckets
Completed. ");
        }
        catch (Exception ex)
        {
            JOptionPane.showMessageDialog(S3Manager.this,"Error Executing List Buckets. "
+ ex.getMessage());
        }
    }
}
```

List Buckets method makes a request and loops through the Buckets in the result. Extracts Bucket Name and Creation Date and updates the buckets jtable.

Let's see the List Objects in Bucket method.

List Objects in Bucket event handler code

```
private class ListObjectsInBucket extends AbstractAction {
    private ListObjectsInBucket() {
        // JFormDesigner - Action initialization - DO NOT MODIFY    //GEN-BEGIN:initComponents
        // Generated using JFormDesigner Evaluation license - Aditya Yadav
        putValue(NAME, "List Objects In Bucket");
        // JFormDesigner - End of action initialization  //GEN-END:initComponents
    }
```

```java
public void actionPerformed(ActionEvent e) {
    try
    {
        S3Service s3 = AmazonClientFactory.getInstance().getS3Service();
        S3Bucket bucket = new S3Bucket();
        bucket.setName(textFieldBucketName.getText());
        S3Object[] objects = s3.listObjects(bucket);
        Object[] columnIdentifiers = new Object[]{"Key", "Last Modified Date"};
        ArrayList data = new ArrayList();

        for (int i=0; i<objects.length; i++){
            data.add(new Object[]{objects[i].getKey(), objects[i].getLastModifiedDate().toString()});
        }
        DefaultTableModel tableModel = (DefaultTableModel)tableS3ObjectsList.getModel();
        tableModel.setDataVector((Object[][])data.toArray(new Object[0][0]), columnIdentifiers);
        JOptionPane.showMessageDialog(S3Manager.this,"List Objects In Bucket Completed. ");
    }
    catch (Exception ex)
    {
```

```
                JOptionPane.showMessageDialog(S3Manager.this,"Error Executing List Objects In Bucket. " + ex.getMessage());

            }

        }

    }
```

This method makes a request with the bucket name and then loops over the S3Objects returned and grabs the Key and LastModified fields and updates the objects jtable.

Let's see the browse method.

Browse event handler code

```
private class Browse extends AbstractAction {

    private Browse() {

        // JFormDesigner - Action initialization - DO NOT MODIFY  //GEN-BEGIN:initComponents

        // Generated using JFormDesigner Evaluation license - Aditya Yadav

        putValue(NAME, "Browse");

        // JFormDesigner - End of action initialization  //GEN-END:initComponents

    }




    public void actionPerformed(ActionEvent e) {

        JFileChooser fc = new JFileChooser();

        fc.setDialogTitle("Select File");

        if (fc.showOpenDialog(S3Manager.this)==JFileChooser.APPROVE_OPTION){

            textFieldFileName.setText(fc.getSelectedFile().getAbsolutePath());
```

```
            }
        }
    }
```

This method opens a JFileChooser and puts the name of the selected file into the File Name text box. Let's see the Delete Bucket method.

Delete Bucket event handler code

```java
private class DeleteBucket extends AbstractAction {

    private DeleteBucket() {

        // JFormDesigner - Action initialization - DO NOT MODIFY  //GEN-BEGIN:initComponents

        // Generated using JFormDesigner Evaluation license - Aditya Yadav

        putValue(NAME, "Delete Bucket");

        // JFormDesigner - End of action initialization  //GEN-END:initComponents

    }

    public void actionPerformed(ActionEvent e) {

        try
        {

            S3Service s3 = AmazonClientFactory.getInstance().getS3Service();

            S3Bucket bucket = new S3Bucket();

            bucket.setName(textFieldBucketName.getText());

            s3.deleteBucket(bucket);
```

```
                JOptionPane.showMessageDialog(S3Manager.this,"Delete Bucket Completed. ");

        }

        catch (Exception ex)

        {

                JOptionPane.showMessageDialog(S3Manager.this,"Error Executing Delete Bucket. " + ex.getMessage());

        }

            }

    }
```

The method makes a delete bucket request with the bucket name and if the bucket is empty it gets deleted.

Let's see the Make Bucket Public method.

Make Bucket Public event handler code

```
private class MakeBucketPublic extends AbstractAction {

        private MakeBucketPublic() {

                // JFormDesigner - Action initialization - DO NOT MODIFY    //GEN-BEGIN:initComponents

                // Generated using JFormDesigner Evaluation license - Aditya Yadav

                putValue(NAME, "Make Bucket Public");

                // JFormDesigner - End of action initialization  //GEN-END:initComponents

        }

        public void actionPerformed(ActionEvent e) {
```

```java
            try
        {
                        S3Service s3 = AmazonClientFactory.getInstance().getS3Service();

                        S3Bucket bucket = s3.getBucket(textFieldBucketName.getText());

                        AccessControlList bucketAcl = s3.getBucketAcl(bucket);

                        bucketAcl.grantPermission(GroupGrantee.ALL_USERS, Permission.PERMISSION_READ);


                        bucket.setAcl(bucketAcl);

                        s3.putBucketAcl(bucket);


                        S3Bucket listBucket = new S3Bucket();

                        listBucket.setName(textFieldBucketName.getText());

                        S3Object[] s3Objects = s3.listObjects(listBucket);


                        for (int i=0; i<s3Objects.length; i++){

                                    AccessControlList objectAcl = s3.getObjectAcl(bucket, s3Objects[i].getKey());

                                        objectAcl.grantPermission(GroupGrantee.ALL_USERS, Permission.PERMISSION_READ);

            s3.putObjectAcl(textFieldBucketName.getText(),s3Objects[i].getKey(), objectAcl);
                        }
                JOptionPane.showMessageDialog(S3Manager.this,"Make Bucket Public Completed. ");
```

```
            }
        catch (Exception ex)
        {
            JOptionPane.showMessageDialog(S3Manager.this,"Error Executing Make Bucket Public. " + ex.getMessage());
        }
        }
    }
```

This method grants Read Permission to All Users to make the bucket and all the objects in it publically readable. It lists all the objects in the current bucket and then for each object sets their ACL.

Let's see the Download Selected Objects method.

Download Selected Objects event handler code

```
private class DownloadSelectedObjects extends AbstractAction {
    private DownloadSelectedObjects() {
        // JFormDesigner - Action initialization - DO NOT MODIFY  //GEN-BEGIN:initComponents
        // Generated using JFormDesigner Evaluation license - Aditya Yadav
        putValue(NAME, "Download Selected Objects");
        // JFormDesigner - End of action initialization  //GEN-END:initComponents
    }



    public void actionPerformed(ActionEvent e) {
```

```java
try
{
    JFileChooser fc = new JFileChooser();
    fc.setDialogTitle("Select Directory To Download To");
    fc.setFileSelectionMode(JFileChooser.DIRECTORIES_ONLY);
    fc.setAcceptAllFileFilterUsed(false);
    if (fc.showOpenDialog(S3Manager.this) == JFileChooser.APPROVE_OPTION) {
        String directory = fc.getSelectedFile().getAbsolutePath();
        JOptionPane.showMessageDialog(S3Manager.this, directory);
        S3Service s3 = AmazonClientFactory.getInstance().getS3Service();
        S3Bucket bucket = new S3Bucket();
        bucket.setName(textFieldBucketName.getText());
        int min = tableS3ObjectsList.getSelectionModel().getMinSelectionIndex();
        int max = tableS3ObjectsList.getSelectionModel().getMaxSelectionIndex();
        if (min != -1 && max != -1){
            for (int i=min; i<= max; i++){
                String key = (String) tableS3ObjectsList.getModel().getValueAt(i,0);
                if (key.indexOf("/") >= 0)
                {
```

```java
                    String path = key.substring(0, key.lastIndexOf("/"));

                    File temp = new File(directory+"/"+path); // Folder path

                    if(!temp.exists()) {

                        temp.mkdirs();

                    }

                }

                S3Object s3Object = s3.getObject(bucket,key);

                InputStream objectStream = s3Object.getDataInputStream();

                FileOutputStream fos = new FileOutputStream(directory+"/"+key);

                byte[] data = new byte[100000];

                int readCount = 0;

                while ((readCount = objectStream.read(data))!= -1){

                        fos.write(data,0,readCount);

                }

                objectStream.close();

                fos.close();

                            }

                        }

                }else {

                        JOptionPane.showMessageDialog(S3Manager.this,"Operation Cancelled. ");

                }

        JOptionPane.showMessageDialog(S3Manager.this,"Download Selected Objects Completed. ");
```

```
                    }
            catch (Exception ex)
            {
                    JOptionPane.showMessageDialog(S3Manager.this,"Error   Executing   Downloads Selected Objects. " + ex.getMessage());
            }
        }
    }
}
```

This method prompts the user to select a folder and then loops over each of the selected objects in the objects jtable. For each of the objects it makes a get object request and reads from the data input strream into a file, in the user selected folder, with the object key as the name. It also creates the folder path if it doesn't exist.

Let's see the Delete Selected Objects method.

Delete Selected Objects event handler code

```
private class DeleteSelectedObjects extends AbstractAction {
        private DeleteSelectedObjects() {
                // JFormDesigner - Action initialization - DO NOT MODIFY  //GEN-BEGIN:initComponents
                // Generated using JFormDesigner Evaluation license - Aditya Yadav
                putValue(NAME, "Delete Selected Objects");
                // JFormDesigner - End of action initialization  //GEN-END:initComponents
        }
```

```java
public void actionPerformed(ActionEvent e) {
    try
    {
        S3Service s3 = AmazonClientFactory.getInstance().getS3Service();
        int min = tableS3ObjectsList.getSelectionModel().getMinSelectionIndex();
        int max = tableS3ObjectsList.getSelectionModel().getMaxSelectionIndex();
        if (min != -1 && max != -1){
            for (int i=min; i<= max; i++){
                String key = (String) tableS3ObjectsList.getModel().getValueAt(i,0);
                s3.deleteObject(textFieldBucketName.getText(), key);
            }
        }
        JOptionPane.showMessageDialog(S3Manager.this,"Delete Selected Objects Completed. ");
    }
    catch (Exception ex)
    {
        JOptionPane.showMessageDialog(S3Manager.this,"Error Executing Delete Selected Objects. " + ex.getMessage());
    }
}
```

```
    }
```

This method loops over each of the selected objects in the objects jtable and makes a delete request with the bucket name and the key for each of the objects.

Using the S3 Manager

Let's open S3 Manager which is provided along with this book and start by creating a bucket. R'ber we have to choose a globally unique name for now let me choose 'aditya8937'. And click Put Bucket. The application will respond with a confirmation that it has been created. Or else it will throw an error which means the Bucket name is not appropriate or not unique in which case you should choose another name. After you get the confirmation click the List Buckets button. Your bucket should appear in the Buckets list view. See Below.

Since this is a fresh bucket it doesn't have any objects. Let's start by creating an object from a small file. Hit the browse button and select a small file. I'm choosing 'c:\setup.log' and entering the key as 'setup.log' this is the key used to identify the object in the bucket. And click Put Object button, after you get a confirmation click the List Objects in Bucket button. The object will show up in the Objects list view. See Below.

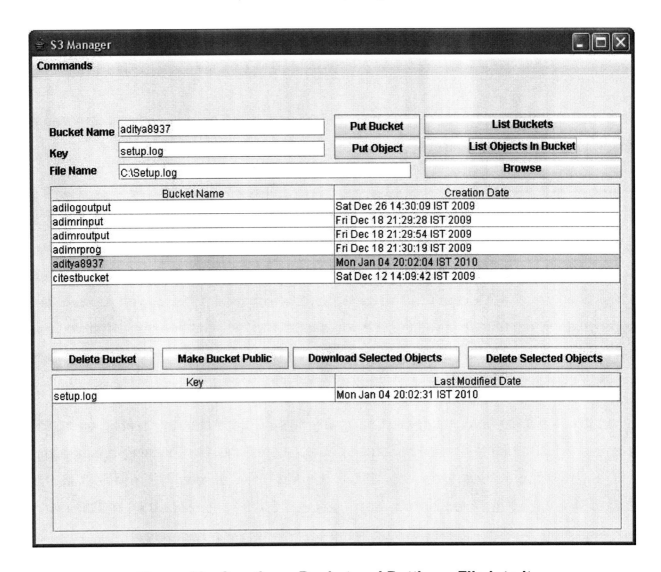

Figure 69 - Creating a Bucket and Putting a File into It

Change the key name to file2.doc in the Key text box, browse and select a doc file and hit Put Object and List Objects in Bucket once again. This will create another object with the doc file as contents with the key file2.doc. So we will have two objects.

Select the file2.doc object in the list view and hit the Delete Selected Objects button. And click List Objects in Bucket button. You will see that it's gone.

Now hit http://<bucketname>.s3.amazonaws.com/setup.log which in our case is http://aditya8937.s3.amazonaws.com/setup.log you will get an access denied message as the object is private. See Below.

Figure 70 - Access Denied Message Accessing the Bucket

Now let's click the Make Bucket Public button. And hit the refresh the object URL. The setup.log file downloads this time. A public bucket can be used to serve as a backend to CloudFront apart from storing your data.

Select the setup.log object in the objects jtable and click on Download Selected Objects. Select Desktop Folder. The setup.log file will get saved onto the desktop.

Now click the delete bucket button. It will throw an exception saying the bucket is not empty. Delete setup.log file by selecting it and click Delete Selected Objects button. And now click Delete Bucket. Click List Buckets and you will see that the bucket is gone.

Retrospective

We saw how to use S3 to store data in the form of objects identified by keys. S3 allows a filesystem to be created using an S3 bucket. This is left as an exercise to the reader.

Chapter 8- Virtual Private Cloud

Amazon Virtual Private Cloud creates a secure seamless bridge between the corporate network and the Amazon cloud. The enterprise can then connect their instances with their enterprise systems over an IPSec VPN connection. AWS uses the ip range you specify for the virtual private cloud. A VPC is an isolated portion of the AWS cloud. A subnet is a segment of the VPC's ip range that the running instances can use; there can be more than one subnet in a VPC. A vpn connection is a connection between the enterprise network and the VPC it has two endpoints, the customer gateway at the end of the enterprise and the VPN gateway at the end of AWS. More than one of your VPC's can be attached to the VPN gateway at AWS end.

Let's look at the Virtual Private Cloud Manager. When finished it looks as shown below.

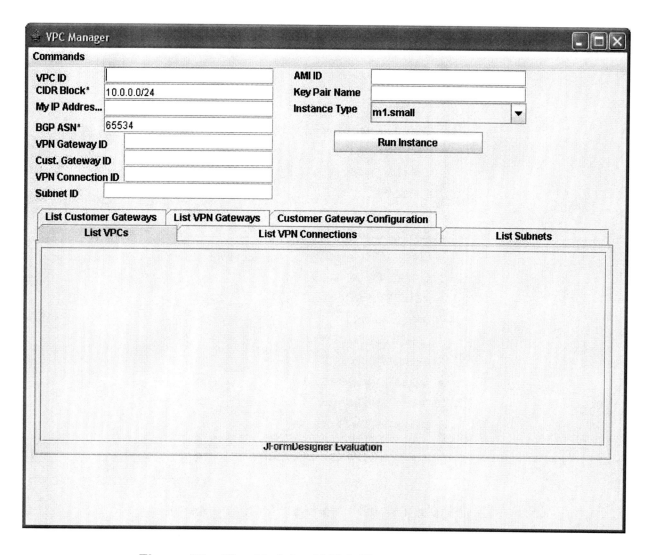

Figure 71 - The Finished VPC Manager Application

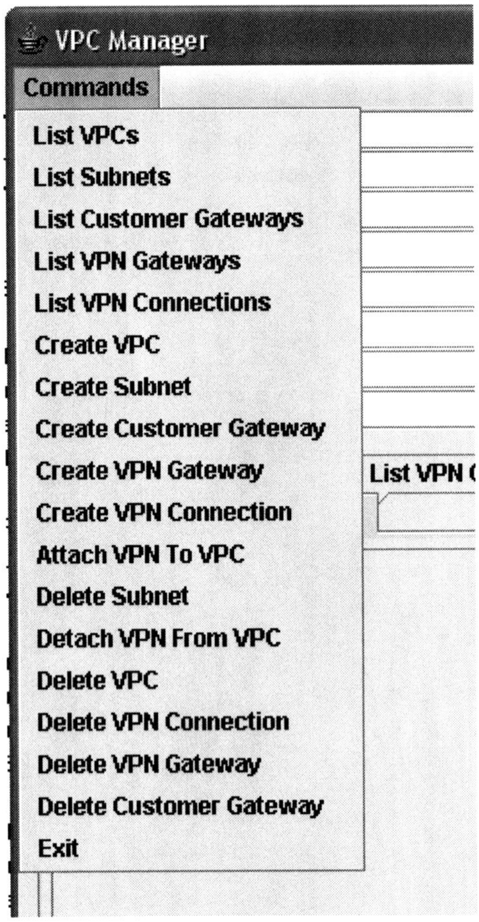

Figure 72 - VPC Manager Menu Items

Let's look at the constructor.

Constructor Code

```java
public VPCManager() {
        initComponents();
        this.setDefaultCloseOperation(JFrame.DO_NOTHING_ON_CLOSE);

        tableListCustomerGateways.getSelectionModel().addListSelectionListener(new
ListSelectionListener(){
            public void valueChanged(ListSelectionEvent e) {
                try {
                    if (!e.getValueIsAdjusting()){
                        String value = (String)
tableListCustomerGateways.getValueAt(tableListCustomerGateways.getSelectedRow(),0);
                        textFieldCustGatewayID.setText(value);
                    }
                } catch (Exception ex){};
            }
        });
        tableListSubnets.getSelectionModel().addListSelectionListener(new
```

```java
ListSelectionListener(){
            public void valueChanged(ListSelectionEvent e) {
                try {
                    if (!e.getValueIsAdjusting()){
                        String value = (String) tableListSubnets.getValueAt(tableListSubnets.getSelectedRow(),0);
                        textFieldSubnetID.setText(value);
                    }
                } catch (Exception ex){};
            }
        });
        tableListVPCs.getSelectionModel().addListSelectionListener(new ListSelectionListener(){
            public void valueChanged(ListSelectionEvent e) {
                try {
                    if (!e.getValueIsAdjusting()){
                        String value = (String) tableListVPCs.getValueAt(tableListVPCs.getSelectedRow(),0);
                        textFieldVPCId.setText(value);
                    }
                } catch (Exception ex){};
            }
        });
        tableListVPNConnections.getSelectionModel().addListSelectionListener(new ListSelectionListener(){
            public void valueChanged(ListSelectionEvent e) {
                try {
                    if (!e.getValueIsAdjusting()){
                        String value = (String) tableListVPNConnections.getValueAt(tableListVPNConnections.getSelectedRow(),0);
                        textFieldVPNConnectionID.setText(value);
                    }
                } catch (Exception ex){};
            }
        });
        tableListVPNGateways.getSelectionModel().addListSelectionListener(new ListSelectionListener(){
            public void valueChanged(ListSelectionEvent e) {
                try {
                    if (!e.getValueIsAdjusting()){
                        String value = (String) tableListVPNGateways.getValueAt(tableListVPNGateways.getSelectedRow(),0);
                        textFieldVPNGatewayID.setText(value);
                    }
                } catch (Exception ex){};
            }
        });
    }
```

The above code setsup all the selection changed event handlers on the JTables so that everytime the selected row/item in the JTables change their respective text boxes are updated with the information. Let's look at the List VPC's event handler shown below.

List VPCs event handler code

```java
private class ListVPCs extends AbstractAction {

    private ListVPCs() {

        // JFormDesigner - Action initialization - DO NOT MODIFY   //GEN-BEGIN:initComponents

        // Generated using JFormDesigner Evaluation license - Aditya Yadav

        putValue(NAME, "LIST VPCs");

        // JFormDesigner - End of action initialization  //GEN-END:initComponents

    }


    public void actionPerformed(ActionEvent e) {

        try {

            AmazonEC2Client ec2 = AmazonClientFactory.getInstance().getEC2Client();

            DescribeVpcsRequest request = new DescribeVpcsRequest();

            DescribeVpcsResponse response = ec2.describeVpcs(request);


            Object[] columnIdentifiers = new Object[] { "ID",

                "State", "CIDR Block"};


            ArrayList data = new ArrayList();
```

```
                for (Vpc vpc : response.getDescribeVpcsResult().getVpc()) {
                    data.add(new Object[] { vpc.getVpcId(),
                        vpc.getVpcState(),
                        vpc.getCidrBlock()
                    });
                }
                DefaultTableModel tableModel = (DefaultTableModel) tableListVPCs.getModel();
                tableModel.setDataVector((Object[][]) data.toArray(new Object[0][0]), columnIdentifiers);
                JOptionPane.showMessageDialog(VPCManager.this, "List VPCs Completed. ");
            } catch (Exception ex) {
                JOptionPane.showMessageDialog(VPCManager.this, "Error Executing List VPCs. " + ex.getMessage());
            }
        }
    }
}
```

The above code makes a describe vpc's request and updates the jtable with vpc id, state and cidr block. Let's look at the Run Instance event handler shown below.

Run Instance event handler code

```
private class RunInstance extends AbstractAction {
```

```java
        private RunInstance() {
                // JFormDesigner - Action initialization - DO NOT MODIFY    //GEN-BEGIN:initComponents
                // Generated using JFormDesigner Evaluation license - Aditya Yadav
                putValue(NAME, "Run Instance");
                // JFormDesigner - End of action initialization  //GEN-END:initComponents
        }


        public void actionPerformed(ActionEvent e) {
            try {
                AmazonEC2Client ec2 = AmazonClientFactory.getInstance().getEC2Client();
                RunInstancesRequest request = new RunInstancesRequest();
    request.setImageId(textFieldAMIId.getText());
    request.setKeyName(textFieldKeyPairName.getText());
    request.setMinCount(1);
    request.setMaxCount(1);
    MonitoringSpecification spec = new MonitoringSpecification();
    spec.setEnabled(true);
    request.setMonitoring(spec);
    request.setInstanceType((String)comboBoxInstanceType.getSelectedItem());
    request.setSubnetId(textFieldSubnetID.getText());
    RunInstancesResponse response = ec2.runInstances(request);
```

```
                    JOptionPane.showMessageDialog(VPCManager.this, "Run Instance
Completed. ");

            } catch (Exception ex) {

                    JOptionPane.showMessageDialog(VPCManager.this,        "Error
Executing Run Instance. " + ex.getMessage());

            }

        }

    }
```

The above code runs one instance with monitoring enabled, of the given instance type and with the given subnet id. This method differs from the one in AMI Builder where we were also launching instances. Here we specify a subnet id and this instance will be launched into the Virtual Private Cloud Subnet that we specify. Look at the List VPN Connections event handler code shown below.

List VPN Connections event handler code

```
private class ListVPNConnections extends AbstractAction {

    private ListVPNConnections() {

        // JFormDesigner - Action initialization - DO NOT MODIFY    //GEN-BEGIN:initComponents

        // Generated using JFormDesigner Evaluation license - Aditya Yadav

        putValue(NAME, "List VPN Connections");

        // JFormDesigner - End of action initialization  //GEN-END:initComponents

    }

    public void actionPerformed(ActionEvent e) {
```

```java
try {
    AmazonEC2Client ec2 = AmazonClientFactory.getInstance().getEC2Client();
    DescribeVpnConnectionsRequest request = new DescribeVpnConnectionsRequest();
    DescribeVpnConnectionsResponse response = ec2.describeVpnConnections(request);

    Object[] columnIdentifiers = new Object[] { "ID",
            "State", "Vpn Gateway ID", "Customer Gateway ID"};

    ArrayList data = new ArrayList();
    for (VpnConnection conn : response.getDescribeVpnConnectionsResult().getVpnConnection()) {
        data.add(new Object[] { conn.getVpnConnectionId() ,
                conn.getVpnConnectionState() ,
                conn.getVpnGatewayId() ,
                conn.getCustomerGatewayId()
        });
    }
    DefaultTableModel tableModel = (DefaultTableModel) tableListVPNConnections.getModel();
    tableModel.setDataVector((Object[][]) data.toArray(new Object[0][0]), columnIdentifiers);
    JOptionPane.showMessageDialog(VPCManager.this, "List Vpn Connections Completed. ");
```

```
                } catch (Exception ex) {
                        JOptionPane.showMessageDialog(VPCManager.this, "Error Executing List Vpn Connections. " + ex.getMessage());
                }
            }
        }
```

This method makes a describe VPN Connections request and iterates through the results and updates the Jtable with vpn connection id, state, vpn gateway id and customer gateway id. Look at the List Subnets event handler code shown below.

List Subnets event handler code

```
private class ListSubnets extends AbstractAction {
        private ListSubnets() {
                // JFormDesigner - Action initialization - DO NOT MODIFY  //GEN-BEGIN:initComponents
                // Generated using JFormDesigner Evaluation license - Aditya Yadav
                putValue(NAME, "List Subnets");
                // JFormDesigner - End of action initialization  //GEN-END:initComponents
        }

        public void actionPerformed(ActionEvent e) {
            try {
                AmazonEC2Client ec2 = AmazonClientFactory.getInstance().getEC2Client();
                DescribeSubnetsRequest request = new
```

```java
DescribeSubnetsRequest();

        DescribeSubnetsResponse response = ec2.describeSubnets(request);


                Object[] columnIdentifiers = new Object[] { "ID",

                    "State", "CIDR Block"};


                ArrayList data = new ArrayList();

                for (Subnet subnet :
response.getDescribeSubnetsResult().getSubnet()) {

                    data.add(new Object[] { subnet.getSubnetId() ,

                        subnet.getSubnetState() ,

                        subnet.getCidrBlock()

                    });

                }

                DefaultTableModel tableModel = (DefaultTableModel)
tableListSubnets.getModel();

                tableModel.setDataVector((Object[][]) data.toArray(new
Object[0][0]), columnIdentifiers);

                JOptionPane.showMessageDialog(VPCManager.this, "List Subnets
Completed. ");

            } catch (Exception ex) {

                JOptionPane.showMessageDialog(VPCManager.this, "Error
Executing List Subnets. " + ex.getMessage());

            }

        }
```

}

This method makes a describe subnets request and updates the JTable with subnet id, state and cidr block of subnets it finds. Look at the List Customer Gateway's event handler code shown below.

List Customer Gateway event handler code

```java
private class ListCustomerGateways extends AbstractAction {

    private ListCustomerGateways() {
        // JFormDesigner - Action initialization - DO NOT MODIFY  //GEN-BEGIN:initComponents
        // Generated using JFormDesigner Evaluation license - Aditya Yadav
        putValue(NAME, "List Customer Gateways");
        // JFormDesigner - End of action initialization  //GEN-END:initComponents
    }

    public void actionPerformed(ActionEvent e) {
        try {
            AmazonEC2Client ec2 = AmazonClientFactory.getInstance().getEC2Client();
            DescribeCustomerGatewaysRequest request = new DescribeCustomerGatewaysRequest();
            DescribeCustomerGatewaysResponse response = ec2.describeCustomerGateways(request);
```

```java
                    Object[] columnIdentifiers = new Object[] { "ID",
                        "State", "IP Address", "Bgp Asn"};

                    ArrayList data = new ArrayList();
                    for (CustomerGateway gateway : response.getDescribeCustomerGatewaysResult().getCustomerGateway()) {
                        data.add(new Object[] { gateway.getCustomerGatewayId() ,
                            gateway.getCustomerGatewayState() ,
                            gateway.getIpAddress(),
                            gateway.getBgpAsn()
                        });
                    }
                    DefaultTableModel tableModel = (DefaultTableModel) tableListCustomerGateways.getModel();
                    tableModel.setDataVector((Object[][]) data.toArray(new Object[0][0]), columnIdentifiers);
                    JOptionPane.showMessageDialog(VPCManager.this, "List Customer Gateways Completed. ");
                } catch (Exception ex) {
                    JOptionPane.showMessageDialog(VPCManager.this, "Error Executing List Customer Gateways. " + ex.getMessage());
                }
            }
        }
```

This method lists the customer gateways by updating the JTable with customer gateway id, state, IP address and bgp asn's. Look at the List VPN Gateway's and its utility method as shown below.

List VPN Gateway event handler code

```
private class ListVPNGateways extends AbstractAction {

    private ListVPNGateways() {

        // JFormDesigner - Action initialization - DO NOT MODIFY   //GEN-BEGIN:initComponents

        // Generated using JFormDesigner Evaluation license - Aditya Yadav

        putValue(NAME, "List VPN Gateways");

        // JFormDesigner - End of action initialization  //GEN-END:initComponents

    }


    public void actionPerformed(ActionEvent e) {

        try {

            AmazonEC2Client ec2 = AmazonClientFactory.getInstance().getEC2Client();

            DescribeVpnGatewaysRequest request = new DescribeVpnGatewaysRequest();

            DescribeVpnGatewaysResponse response = ec2.describeVpnGateways(request);



            Object[] columnIdentifiers = new Object[] { "ID",

                "State", "Vpc Attachments"};
```

```java
            ArrayList data = new ArrayList();
            for (VpnGateway gateway : response.getDescribeVpnGatewaysResult().getVpnGateway()) {
                data.add(new Object[] { gateway.getVpnGatewayId() ,
                    gateway.getVpnGatewayState() ,
                    ConcatenateAttachments(gateway.getVpcAttachment())
                });
            }
            DefaultTableModel tableModel = (DefaultTableModel) tableListVPNGateways.getModel();
            tableModel.setDataVector((Object[][]) data.toArray(new Object[0][0]), columnIdentifiers);
            JOptionPane.showMessageDialog(VPCManager.this, "List VPN Gateways Completed. ");
        } catch (Exception ex) {
            JOptionPane.showMessageDialog(VPCManager.this, "Error Executing List VPN Gateways. " + ex.getMessage());
        }
    }

    private String ConcatenateAttachments(List<VpcAttachment> list)
    {
        String result = "";
        for (VpcAttachment attachment : list)
```

```
        {

            result = result + attachment.getVpcId() + ",";

        }

        return result;

    }


}
```

This method lists the VPN Gateways and populates the JTable with vpn gateway id, state and the vpc's attached to it. The utility method converts a list of vpc's into a comma separated names in a string. Look at the Create VPC method shown below.

Create VPC event handler code

```
private class CreateVPC extends AbstractAction {

    private CreateVPC() {

        // JFormDesigner - Action initialization - DO NOT MODIFY  //GEN-BEGIN:initComponents

        // Generated using JFormDesigner Evaluation license - Aditya Yadav

        putValue(NAME, "Create VPC");

        // JFormDesigner - End of action initialization  //GEN-END:initComponents

    }



    public void actionPerformed(ActionEvent e) {

        try {

            AmazonEC2Client            ec2            =
```

```
AmazonClientFactory.getInstance().getEC2Client();

            CreateVpcRequest vpcRequest = new CreateVpcRequest();

    vpcRequest.setCidrBlock(textFieldCIDRBlock.getText());

    CreateVpcResponse vpcResponse = ec2.createVpc(vpcRequest);

    textFieldVPCId.setText(vpcResponse.getCreateVpcResult().getVpc().getVpcId());

    JOptionPane.showMessageDialog(VPCManager.this, "Create VPC Completed. ");

        } catch (Exception ex) {

            JOptionPane.showMessageDialog(VPCManager.this,        "Error
Executing Create VPC. " + ex.getMessage());

        }

    }

}
```

This method creates a VPC with the given CIDR block range and updates the vpc id returned into its text field which can then be used by other methods. Look at the Create Subnet code shown below.

Create Subnet event handler code

```
private class CreateSubnet extends AbstractAction {

    private CreateSubnet() {

        // JFormDesigner - Action initialization - DO NOT MODIFY    //GEN-BEGIN:initComponents

        // Generated using JFormDesigner Evaluation license - Aditya Yadav

        putValue(NAME, "Create Subnet");

        // JFormDesigner - End of action initialization  //GEN-END:initComponents
```

```java
            }


            public void actionPerformed(ActionEvent e) {

                try {

                    AmazonEC2Client ec2 = AmazonClientFactory.getInstance().getEC2Client();

                    CreateSubnetRequest csRequest = new CreateSubnetRequest();

                    csRequest.setVpcId(textFieldVPCId.getText());

                    csRequest.setCidrBlock(textFieldCIDRBlock.getText());

                    CreateSubnetResponse csResponse = ec2.createSubnet(csRequest);

                    textFieldSubnetID.setText(csResponse.getCreateSubnetResult().getSubnet().getSubnetId());

                    JOptionPane.showMessageDialog(VPCManager.this, "Create Subnet Completed. ");

                } catch (Exception ex) {

                    JOptionPane.showMessageDialog(VPCManager.this, "Error Executing Create Subnet. " + ex.getMessage());

                }

            }

        }
```

This method creates a subnet in the vpc with the id given and with the cidr block range given. If there is one subnet the cidr block range of the vpc and the subnet will be the same or else the subnet will need a portion of the vpc cidr block. Look at the Create Customer Gateway method shown below.

Create Customer Gateway event handler code

```java
private class CreateCustomerGateway extends AbstractAction {

    private CreateCustomerGateway() {

        // JFormDesigner - Action initialization - DO NOT MODIFY     //GEN-BEGIN:initComponents

        // Generated using JFormDesigner Evaluation license - Aditya Yadav

        putValue(NAME, "Create Customer Gateway");

        // JFormDesigner - End of action initialization  //GEN-END:initComponents

    }


    public void actionPerformed(ActionEvent e) {

        try {

            AmazonEC2Client ec2 = AmazonClientFactory.getInstance().getEC2Client();

            CreateCustomerGatewayRequest ccgRequest = new CreateCustomerGatewayRequest();

            ccgRequest.setType("ipsec.1");

            ccgRequest.setBgpAsn(Integer.parseInt(textFieldBGPAsn.getText()));

            ccgRequest.setIpAddress(textFieldMyIPAddress.getText());

            CreateCustomerGatewayResponse ccgResponse = ec2.createCustomerGateway(ccgRequest);


            textFieldCustGatewayID.setText(ccgResponse.getCreateCustomerGatewayResult().getCustomerGateway().getCustomerGatewayId());

            JOptionPane.showMessageDialog(VPCManager.this, "Create Customer Gateway Completed. ");

        } catch (Exception ex) {
```

```
                    JOptionPane.showMessageDialog(VPCManager.this,         "Error
Executing Create Customer Gateway. " + ex.getMessage());

                }

            }

        }
```

This method creates a customer gateway with the given bgp asn, public ip address of the type ipsec.1. Look at the Create VPN Gateway method shown below.

Create VPN Gateway event handler code

```
private class CreateVPNGateway extends AbstractAction {

        private CreateVPNGateway() {

            // JFormDesigner - Action initialization - DO NOT MODIFY  //GEN-BEGIN:initComponents

            // Generated using JFormDesigner Evaluation license - Aditya Yadav

            putValue(NAME, "Create VPN Gateway");

            // JFormDesigner - End of action initialization  //GEN-END:initComponents

        }



        public void actionPerformed(ActionEvent e) {

            try {

                AmazonEC2Client                ec2                =
AmazonClientFactory.getInstance().getEC2Client();

                CreateVpnGatewayRequest        cvgRequest         =        new
CreateVpnGatewayRequest();

        cvgRequest.setType("ipsec.1");
```

```
            CreateVpnGatewayResponse cvgResponse = ec2.createVpnGateway(cvgRequest);

textFieldVPNGatewayID.setText(cvgResponse.getCreateVpnGatewayResult().getVpnGateway().getVpnGatewayId());

            JOptionPane.showMessageDialog(VPCManager.this, "Create VPN Gateway Completed.");

                } catch (Exception ex) {

                    JOptionPane.showMessageDialog(VPCManager.this, "Error Executing Create VPN Gateway. " + ex.getMessage());

                }

            }

        }
```

This method creates a VPN Gateway of the type ipsec.1. Look at the Create VPN Connection method shown below.

Create VPN Connection event handler code

```
private class CreateVPNConnection extends AbstractAction {

        private CreateVPNConnection() {

            // JFormDesigner - Action initialization - DO NOT MODIFY  //GEN-BEGIN:initComponents

            // Generated using JFormDesigner Evaluation license - Aditya Yadav

            putValue(NAME, "Create VPN Connection");

            // JFormDesigner - End of action initialization  //GEN-END:initComponents

        }
```

```java
public void actionPerformed(ActionEvent e) {
    try {
        AmazonEC2Client ec2 = AmazonClientFactory.getInstance().getEC2Client();

        CreateVpnConnectionRequest cvcRequest = new CreateVpnConnectionRequest();

        cvcRequest.setType("ipsec.1");

        cvcRequest.setVpnGatewayId(textFieldVPNGatewayID.getText());

        cvcRequest.setCustomerGatewayId(textFieldCustGatewayID.getText());

        //cvcRequest.Format = "cisco-ios-isr";//generic, cisco-ios-isr, or juniper-junos-j

        CreateVpnConnectionResponse cvcResponse = ec2.createVpnConnection(cvcRequest);

        textFieldVPNConnectionID.setText(cvcResponse.getCreateVpnConnectionResult().getVpnConnection().getVpnConnectionId());

        textPaneCustomerGatewayConfiguration.setText(cvcResponse.getCreateVpnConnectionResult().getVpnConnection().getCustomerGatewayConfiguration());

        writeToFile(textFieldVPNConnectionID.getText() + ".xml", textPaneCustomerGatewayConfiguration.getText());

        TransformerFactory tFactory = TransformerFactory.newInstance();

        Transformer transformer = tFactory.newTransformer(new StreamSource("customer-gateway-cisco-ios-isr.xslt"));

        transformer.transform(new StreamSource(textFieldVPNConnectionID.getText() + ".xml"),new StreamResult( new FileOutputStream(textFieldVPNConnectionID.getText() + ".cisco")));

        transformer = tFactory.newTransformer(new StreamSource("customer-gateway-juniper-junos-j.xslt"));

        transformer.transform(new StreamSource(textFieldVPNConnectionID.getText() +
```

```
".xml"),new    StreamResult(   new    FileOutputStream(textFieldVPNConnectionID.getText()   +
".juniper")));

        transformer   =   tFactory.newTransformer(new   StreamSource("customer-gateway-
generic.xslt"));

        transformer.transform(new    StreamSource(textFieldVPNConnectionID.getText()   +
".xml"),new    StreamResult(   new    FileOutputStream(textFieldVPNConnectionID.getText()   +
".generic")));


        JOptionPane.showMessageDialog(VPCManager.this,   "Create   VPN   Connection
Completed. ");

            } catch (Exception ex) {

                JOptionPane.showMessageDialog(VPCManager.this,   "Error
Executing Create VPN Connection. " + ex.getMessage());

            }

        }

    }
```

This method creates a VPN Connection of the type ipsec.1 and with the given VPN Gateway and Customer Gateway. It then saves the raw configuration into a file and then runs 3 xslt transforms on it, one each to convert the raw configuration into Cisco, Juniper and Generic formats. Look at the Attach VPN to VPC method shown below.

Attach VPN to VPC event handler code

```
private class AttachVPNToVPC extends AbstractAction {

        private AttachVPNToVPC() {

                // JFormDesigner  -  Action  initialization  - DO NOT MODIFY    //GEN-
BEGIN:initComponents
```

```java
// Generated using JFormDesigner Evaluation license - Aditya Yadav
putValue(NAME, "Attach VPN To VPC");
// JFormDesigner - End of action initialization  //GEN-END:initComponents
}


public void actionPerformed(ActionEvent e) {
    try {
        AmazonEC2Client ec2 = AmazonClientFactory.getInstance().getEC2Client();
        AttachVpnGatewayRequest avgRequest = new AttachVpnGatewayRequest();
        avgRequest.setVpcId(textFieldVPCId.getText());
        avgRequest.setVpnGatewayId(textFieldVPNGatewayID.getText());
        AttachVpnGatewayResponse avgResponse = ec2.attachVpnGateway(avgRequest);
        JOptionPane.showMessageDialog(VPCManager.this, "Attach VPN to VPC Completed. ");
    } catch (Exception ex) {
        JOptionPane.showMessageDialog(VPCManager.this, "Error Executing Attach VPN to VPC. " + ex.getMessage());
    }
}
```

This method attaches the given Vpn Gateway to the given Vpc. Look at the Delete Subnet method shown below.

Delete Subnet event handler code

```java
private class DeleteSubnet extends AbstractAction {

    private DeleteSubnet() {
        // JFormDesigner - Action initialization - DO NOT MODIFY  //GEN-BEGIN:initComponents
        // Generated using JFormDesigner Evaluation license - Aditya Yadav
        putValue(NAME, "Delete Subnet");
        // JFormDesigner - End of action initialization  //GEN-END:initComponents
    }


    public void actionPerformed(ActionEvent e) {
        try {
            AmazonEC2Client ec2 = AmazonClientFactory.getInstance().getEC2Client();
            DeleteSubnetRequest dsRequest = new DeleteSubnetRequest();
            dsRequest.setSubnetId(textFieldSubnetID.getText());
            DeleteSubnetResponse dsResponse = ec2.deleteSubnet(dsRequest);
            JOptionPane.showMessageDialog(VPCManager.this, "Delete Subnet Completed. ");
        } catch (Exception ex) {
            JOptionPane.showMessageDialog(VPCManager.this, "Error Executing Delete Subnet. " + ex.getMessage());
        }
    }
}
```

This method deletes the subnet with the given subnet id. Look at the Detach VPN from VPC method shown below.

Detach VPN from VPC event handler code

```java
private class DetachVPNFromVPC extends AbstractAction {

    private DetachVPNFromVPC() {

        // JFormDesigner - Action initialization - DO NOT MODIFY  //GEN-BEGIN:initComponents

        // Generated using JFormDesigner Evaluation license - Aditya Yadav

        putValue(NAME, "Detach VPN From VPC");

        // JFormDesigner - End of action initialization  //GEN-END:initComponents

    }


    public void actionPerformed(ActionEvent e) {

        try {

            AmazonEC2Client ec2 = AmazonClientFactory.getInstance().getEC2Client();

            DetachVpnGatewayRequest dgRequest = new DetachVpnGatewayRequest();

            dgRequest.setVpcId(textFieldVPCId.getText());

            dgRequest.setVpnGatewayId(textFieldVPNGatewayID.getText());

            DetachVpnGatewayResponse dgResponse = ec2.detachVpnGateway(dgRequest);

            JOptionPane.showMessageDialog(VPCManager.this, "Detach VPN from VPC Completed.");

        } catch (Exception ex) {

            JOptionPane.showMessageDialog(VPCManager.this, "Error
```

```
Executing Detach VPN from VPC. " + ex.getMessage());
                }
            }
        }
```

This method detaches the given vpc from the given vpn gateway. Look at the Delete VPC method as shown below.

Delete VPC event handler code

```java
private class DeleteVPC extends AbstractAction {

    private DeleteVPC() {
        // JFormDesigner - Action initialization - DO NOT MODIFY  //GEN-BEGIN:initComponents
        // Generated using JFormDesigner Evaluation license - Aditya Yadav
        putValue(NAME, "Delete VPC");
        // JFormDesigner - End of action initialization  //GEN-END:initComponents
    }

    public void actionPerformed(ActionEvent e) {
        try {
            AmazonEC2Client ec2 = AmazonClientFactory.getInstance().getEC2Client();
            DeleteVpcRequest dvpcRequest = new DeleteVpcRequest();
            dvpcRequest.setVpcId(textFieldVPCId.getText());
            DeleteVpcResponse dvpcResponse = ec2.deleteVpc(dvpcRequest);
```

```
                JOptionPane.showMessageDialog(VPCManager.this, "Delete VPC Completed. ");

            } catch (Exception ex) {

                JOptionPane.showMessageDialog(VPCManager.this,                "Error Executing Delete VPC. " + ex.getMessage());

            }

        }

    }
```

This method deletes the vpc with the given vpc id. Look at the Delete VPN Connection method shown below.

Delete VPN Connection event handler code

```
private class DeleteVPNConnection extends AbstractAction {

        private DeleteVPNConnection() {

            // JFormDesigner - Action initialization - DO NOT MODIFY    //GEN-BEGIN:initComponents

            // Generated using JFormDesigner Evaluation license - Aditya Yadav

            putValue(NAME, "Delete VPN Connection");

            // JFormDesigner - End of action initialization  //GEN-END:initComponents

        }




        public void actionPerformed(ActionEvent e) {

            try {

                AmazonEC2Client            ec2            = AmazonClientFactory.getInstance().getEC2Client();

                DeleteVpnConnectionRequest     dvpncRequest     =     new
```

```
            DeleteVpnConnectionRequest();

                dvpncRequest.setVpnConnectionId(textFieldVPNConnectionID.getText());

                DeleteVpnConnectionResponse        dvpncResponse        =
ec2.deleteVpnConnection(dvpncRequest);

                    JOptionPane.showMessageDialog(VPCManager.this, "Delete VPN
Connection Completed. ");

                } catch (Exception ex) {

                    JOptionPane.showMessageDialog(VPCManager.this,        "Error
Executing Delete VPN Connection. " + ex.getMessage());

                }

            }

        }
```

This method deletes the vpn connection with the given vpn connection id. Look at the Delete VPN Gateway shown below.

Delete VPN Gateway event handler code

```
private class DeleteVPNGateway extends AbstractAction {

        private DeleteVPNGateway() {

            // JFormDesigner - Action initialization - DO NOT MODIFY    //GEN-BEGIN:initComponents

            // Generated using JFormDesigner Evaluation license - Aditya Yadav

            putValue(NAME, "Delete VPN Gateway");

            // JFormDesigner - End of action initialization  //GEN-END:initComponents

        }
```

```java
public void actionPerformed(ActionEvent e) {
    try {
        AmazonEC2Client ec2 = AmazonClientFactory.getInstance().getEC2Client();
        DeleteVpnGatewayRequest dvpngRequest = new DeleteVpnGatewayRequest();
        dvpngRequest.setVpnGatewayId(textFieldVPNGatewayID.getText());
        DeleteVpnGatewayResponse dvpngResponse = ec2.deleteVpnGateway(dvpngRequest);
        JOptionPane.showMessageDialog(VPCManager.this, "Delete VPN Gateway Completed. ");
    } catch (Exception ex) {
        JOptionPane.showMessageDialog(VPCManager.this, "Error Executing Delete VPN Gateway. " + ex.getMessage());
    }
}
```

This method deletes the given VPN Gateway with the given id. Look at the Delete Customer Gateway method shown below.

Delete Customer Gateway event handler code

```java
private class DeleteCustomerGateway extends AbstractAction {
    private DeleteCustomerGateway() {
        // JFormDesigner - Action initialization - DO NOT MODIFY  //GEN-BEGIN:initComponents
        // Generated using JFormDesigner Evaluation license - Aditya Yadav
```

```java
            putValue(NAME, "Delete Customer Gateway");
        // JFormDesigner - End of action initialization  //GEN-END:initComponents
        }


        public void actionPerformed(ActionEvent e) {
            try {
                AmazonEC2Client ec2 = AmazonClientFactory.getInstance().getEC2Client();
                DeleteCustomerGatewayRequest dcgRequest = new DeleteCustomerGatewayRequest();
                dcgRequest.setCustomerGatewayId(textFieldCustGatewayID.getText());
                DeleteCustomerGatewayResponse dcgResponse = ec2.deleteCustomerGateway(dcgRequest);

                JOptionPane.showMessageDialog(VPCManager.this, "Delete Customer Gateway Completed. ");
            } catch (Exception ex) {
                JOptionPane.showMessageDialog(VPCManager.this, "Error Executing Delete Customer Gateway. " + ex.getMessage());
            }
        }
    }
```

This method deletes the Customer Gateway with the given id. We are all set, let's build the project and try it out in the next section.

Using VPC Manager

Find out the public ip of your cisco/juniper/other router. And enter that in the My IP Address text box. We don't have one so we will enter anything just so that we can do a dry run e.g. 122.77.180.99. Click Commands->Create VPC and then click Commands->List VPC's as shown below. The VPC has been created and shows up.

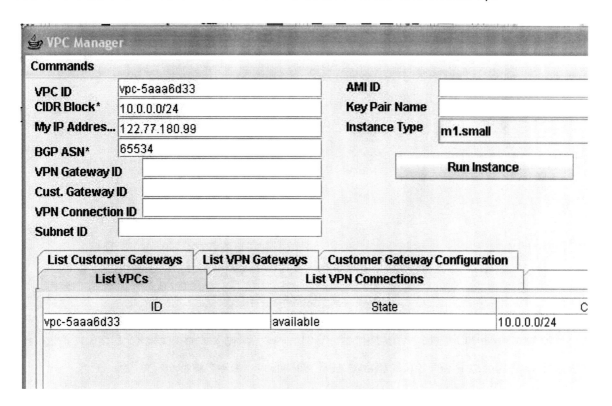

Figure 73 - Create VPC

Now click Commands->Create Subnet and then click Commands->List Subnets. The subnet will get created and will show up as shown below.

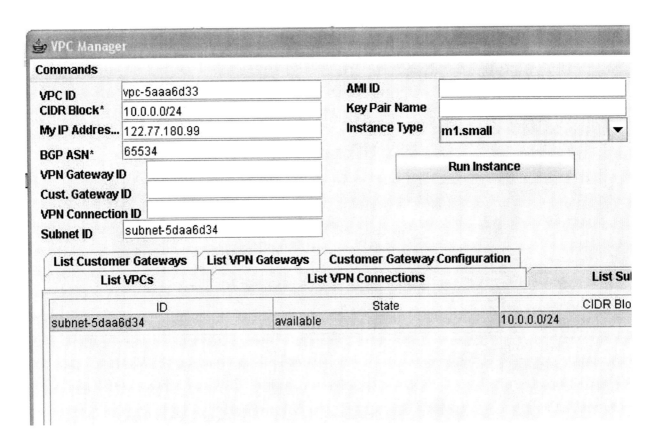

Figure 74 - Create Subnet

Click Commands->Create Customer Gateway and then click Commands->List Customer Gateways it will get created and will show up as shown below.

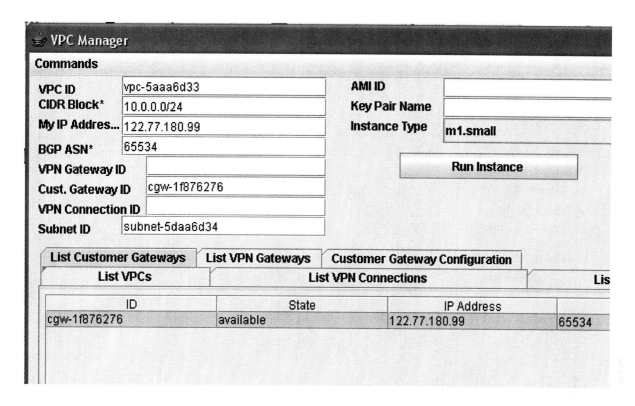

Figure 75 - Create Customer Gateway

Click Commands->Create VPN Gateway and then click Commands->List VPN Gateways it will get created and will show up as shown below. It will take about 2 minutes to become available.

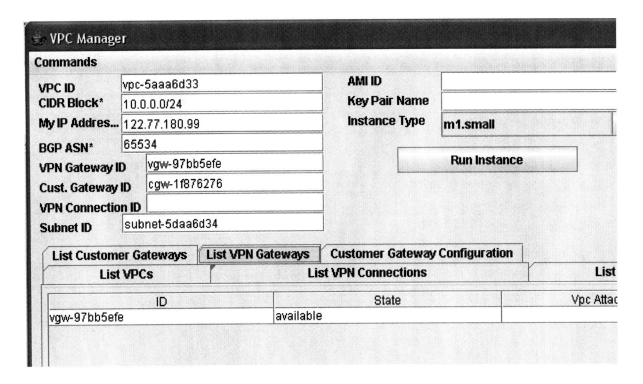

Figure 76 - Create VPN Gateway

Click Commands->Create VPN Connection and then click Commands->List VPN Connections. The VPN connection will get created and will showup as available in 2 minutes, as shown below.

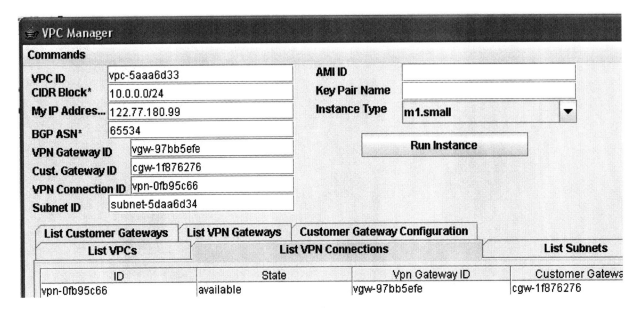

Figure 77 - Create VPN Connection

Now let's attach the VPN Gateway to the VPC. Click Commands->Attach VPN to VPC and click Commands->List VPN Gateway's it will show up as connected to the VPC as shown below.

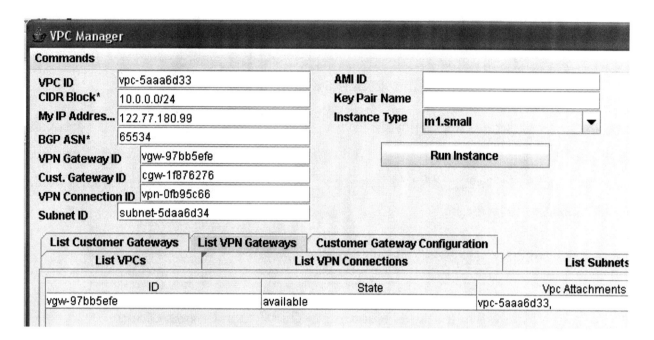

Figure 78 - Attach VPN to VPC

The configuration for our router has been saved in the directory of the program with the file extension .cisco/.juniper/.generic hand over the appropriate file to your network administrator so that he can configure the router.

Let's launch an instance in our virtual private cloud. We have made an AMI earlier so we will enter that ami image id into the text box, along with our KeyPair Name and select instance type as 'm1.small' and click Run Instance button. As shown below.

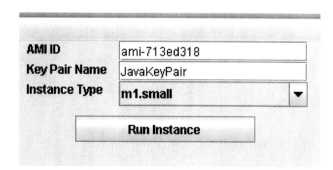

Figure 79 - Run Instance in Our Virtual Private Cloud

Copyright © 2009 by Aditya Yadav (http://adityayadav.com)

Open the AWS EC2 Console, Instances Section and click Show/Hide and select the following columns. As shown below.

Figure 80- Select Columns

The instance shows up with a private ip, no public dns or security group. This instance is in your virtual private cloud. If your network administrator has setup your router you will be able to ping it and access its website with http://10.0.0.4:8080/AWSToolkitDemo/index.jsp

Figure 81 - Instance Running In Our Virtual Private Cloud

Your virtual private cloud is all set. This chapter is over. Don't forget to shutdown everything in the order given below.

1. Shutdown all running instances in the VPC
2. Delete Subnet
3. Detach VPN From VPC
4. Delete VPC
5. Delete VPN Connection
6. Delete VPN Gateway
7. Delete Customer Gateway

Your virtual private cloud will be deleted.

Retrospective

We configured a Virtual Private cloud on Amazon Web Services Cloud. We ran an instance in our VPC and we got our router configured at our end by our network administrator using the configuration files that were generated by the VPC Manager. We accessed the Website on the running instance. And then we shut everything down and deleted the Virtual Private Cloud. The reader should use the subnet id parameter in the excercises shown in the LoadBalancing and AutoScaling chapter and create AutoScaled LoadBalancers on the Virtual Private Cloud.

Chapter 9- SimpleDB

SimpleDB is a service that allows us to store, process and query structured data sets in AWS. There are no entity relationships in SimpleDB. Items are stored in domains and can have arbitrary attributes. No schema needs to be defined and indexes are generated automatically. Access is through a simplistic API and a simple SQL like query language. Users get access to a ready to use cloud scale structured storage without any explicit performance tuning. SimpleDB works in realtime and the data structure can be incrementally changed at anytime.

We are going to look at a SimpleDB Manager. The finished application looks like below.

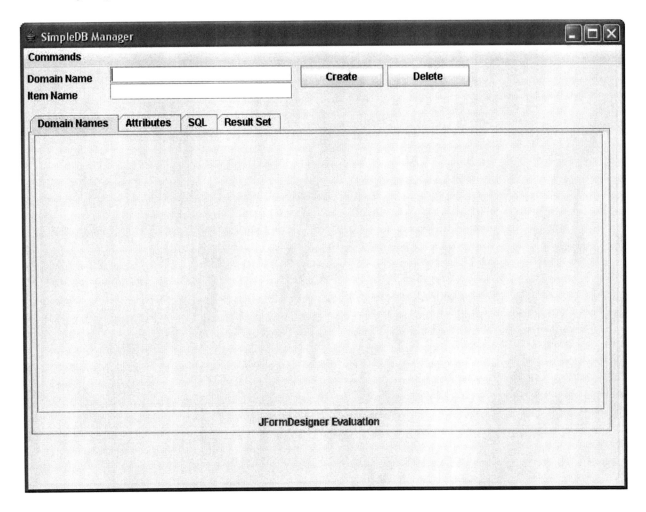

Figure 82 - The Finished SimpleDB Manager Application

The menu items are as shown below.

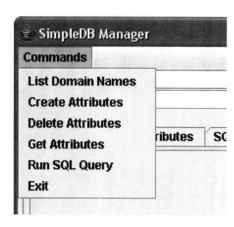

Figure 83 - SimpleDB Manager Menu

The tab control on the form contains 4 tabs each with a JTable except for the SQL tab which contains a JTextPane.

The constructor is shown below.

```
Constructor code

public SimpleDB() {
            initComponents();
            this.setDefaultCloseOperation(JFrame.DO_NOTHING_ON_CLOSE);

            Object[] columnIdentifiers = new Object[]{"Name","Value"};
            ArrayList data = new ArrayList();
    for (int i=0;i<100;i++) data.add(new Object[]{"",""});
            DefaultTableModel tableModel = (DefaultTableModel) tableAttributes.getModel();
            tableModel.setDataVector((Object[][]) data.toArray(new Object[0][0]), columnIdentifiers);

            tableDomainNames.getSelectionModel().addListSelectionListener(new
ListSelectionListener(){
                    public void valueChanged(ListSelectionEvent e) {
                        try {
                            if (!e.getValueIsAdjusting()){
                                String domainName = (String)
tableDomainNames.getValueAt(tableDomainNames.getSelectedRow(),0);
                                textFieldDomainName.setText(domainName);
                            }
                        } catch (Exception ex){};
                    }
            });

            tableResultSet.getSelectionModel().addListSelectionListener(new
ListSelectionListener(){
                    public void valueChanged(ListSelectionEvent e) {
                        try {
                            if (!e.getValueIsAdjusting()){
```

```
                        String itemName = (String)
tableResultSet.getValueAt(tableResultSet.getSelectedRow(),0);
                        textFieldItemName.setText(itemName);
                }
            } catch (Exception ex){};
        }
    });
}
```

The constructor does a couple of things. It prepopulates the attributes jtable with 100 rows with empty strings as Name and Value's. It sets up listeners so that when the domain names jtable selection changes it updates the domain name text field with the domain name of the selected row. It also updates the item name text field when the item selection in the result set jtable changes.

Look at the create button event handler as shown below.

Create Domain event handler code

```
private class CreateDomain extends AbstractAction {

    private CreateDomain() {

        // JFormDesigner - Action initialization - DO NOT MODIFY  //GEN-BEGIN:initComponents

        // Generated using JFormDesigner Evaluation license - Aditya Yadav

        putValue(NAME, "Create");

        // JFormDesigner - End of action initialization  //GEN-END:initComponents

    }




    public void actionPerformed(ActionEvent e) {

        try {

            AmazonSimpleDBClient                    sdb                    =
```

```
AmazonClientFactory.getInstance().getSimpleDBClient();


                    CreateDomainRequest request = new CreateDomainRequest();

    request.setDomainName(textFieldDomainName.getText());

    CreateDomainResponse response = sdb.createDomain(request);


                    JOptionPane.showMessageDialog(SimpleDB.this,"Create   Domain
Completed. ");
                } catch (Exception ex) {
                    JOptionPane.showMessageDialog(SimpleDB.this,"Error   Executing
Create Domain. " + ex.getMessage());
                }
            }
        }
```

The above code makes a create domain request with the domain name desired. Let's see the delete domain event handler as shown below.

Delete Domain event handler code

```
private class DeleteDomain extends AbstractAction {
        private DeleteDomain() {
            // JFormDesigner - Action initialization - DO NOT MODIFY   //GEN-BEGIN:initComponents
            // Generated using JFormDesigner Evaluation license - Aditya Yadav
```

```java
                putValue(NAME, "Delete");

            // JFormDesigner - End of action initialization  //GEN-END:initComponents

        }


        public void actionPerformed(ActionEvent e) {

            try {

                AmazonSimpleDBClient sdb = AmazonClientFactory.getInstance().getSimpleDBClient();


                DeleteDomainRequest request = new DeleteDomainRequest();

    request.setDomainName(textFieldDomainName.getText());

    DeleteDomainResponse response = sdb.deleteDomain(request);


                JOptionPane.showMessageDialog(SimpleDB.this,"Delete Domain Completed. ");

            } catch (Exception ex) {

                JOptionPane.showMessageDialog(SimpleDB.this,"Error Executing Delete Domain. " + ex.getMessage());

            }

        }

    }
```

The above code makes a delete domain request with the name of the domain which is to be deleted. Look at the list domain names event handler shown below.

List Domain Names event handler code

```java
private class ListDomainNames extends AbstractAction {

    private ListDomainNames() {

        // JFormDesigner - Action initialization - DO NOT MODIFY     //GEN-BEGIN:initComponents

        // Generated using JFormDesigner Evaluation license - Aditya Yadav

        putValue(NAME, "List Domain Names");

        // JFormDesigner - End of action initialization  //GEN-END:initComponents

    }


    public void actionPerformed(ActionEvent e) {

        try {

            AmazonSimpleDBClient sdb = AmazonClientFactory.getInstance().getSimpleDBClient();




            ListDomainsRequest request = new ListDomainsRequest();
            ListDomainsResponse response = sdb.listDomains(request);


            Object[] columnIdentifiers = new Object[]{"Domain Name"};


            ArrayList data = new ArrayList();
            for (String domainName : response.getListDomainsResult().getDomainName())
            {
```

```
                data.add(new Object[]{domainName});
            }
            DefaultTableModel tableModel = (DefaultTableModel) tableDomainNames.getModel();
            tableModel.setDataVector((Object[][]) data.toArray(new Object[0][0]), columnIdentifiers);
            JOptionPane.showMessageDialog(SimpleDB.this, "List Domains Completed. ");
        } catch (Exception ex) {
            JOptionPane.showMessageDialog(SimpleDB.this, "Error Executing List Domains. " + ex.getMessage());
        }
    }
}
```

The method makes a list domains request and iterates over the results and updates the jtable with the names of the domains. Look at the Run SQL Query event handler shown below.

Run SQL Query event handler code

```
private class RunSQLQuery extends AbstractAction {
    private RunSQLQuery() {
        // JFormDesigner - Action initialization - DO NOT MODIFY  //GEN-BEGIN:initComponents
        // Generated using JFormDesigner Evaluation license - Aditya Yadav
        putValue(NAME, "Run SQL Query");
```

```java
        // JFormDesigner - End of action initialization  //GEN-END:initComponents
    }



    public void actionPerformed(ActionEvent e) {
        try {
            AmazonSimpleDBClient sdb = AmazonClientFactory.getInstance().getSimpleDBClient();




            SelectRequest request = new SelectRequest();
            request.setSelectExpression(textPaneSQL.getText());
            SelectResponse response = sdb.select(request);
            Object[] columnIdentifiers = new Object[100];
            columnIdentifiers[0]="Item Name";
            for (int i=1;i<100;i++) columnIdentifiers[i]=i+"";


            ArrayList data = new ArrayList();
            for (Item item : response.getSelectResult().getItem())
            {

                String[] values = new String[item.getAttribute().size()+1];
                values[0] = item.getName();
                int i = 1;
                for(Attribute attribute : item.getAttribute())
```

```
            {
                values[i] = attribute.getName()+"="+attribute.getValue();
                i++;
            }
            data.add(values);
        }
        DefaultTableModel tableModel = (DefaultTableModel) tableResultSet.getModel();
        tableModel.setDataVector((Object[][]) data.toArray(new Object[0][0]), columnIdentifiers);
        JOptionPane.showMessageDialog(SimpleDB.this, "Run SQL Query Completed. ");
    } catch (Exception ex) {
        JOptionPane.showMessageDialog(SimpleDB.this, "Error Executing Run SQL Query. " + ex.getMessage());
    }
  }
}
```

The above code creates a 100 column headers with the first one as "Item Name" and from then on named 1 through 99. It takes the user entered SQL and executes the query and then loops over the records returned. It displays the Item Name and all the attributes in the Result Set jtable. Look at the create attributes event handler shown below.

Create Attributes event handler code

```java
private class CreateAttributes extends AbstractAction {

    private CreateAttributes() {

        // JFormDesigner - Action initialization - DO NOT MODIFY    //GEN-BEGIN:initComponents

        // Generated using JFormDesigner Evaluation license - Aditya Yadav

        putValue(NAME, "Create Attributes");

        // JFormDesigner - End of action initialization  //GEN-END:initComponents

    }


    public void actionPerformed(ActionEvent e) {

        try {

            AmazonSimpleDBClient sdb = AmazonClientFactory.getInstance().getSimpleDBClient();


            PutAttributesRequest request = new PutAttributesRequest();

            request.setItemName(textFieldItemName.getText());

            request.setDomainName(textFieldDomainName.getText());

            for (int i=0; i<tableAttributes.getModel().getRowCount();i++)

            {

                String name = (String)tableAttributes.getModel().getValueAt(i,0);

                String value = (String)tableAttributes.getModel().getValueAt(i,1);

                if (!name.trim().equals("") || !value.trim().equals("")){

                    ReplaceableAttribute attribute = new ReplaceableAttribute();

                    attribute.setName(name);
```

```
                attribute.setValue(value);

                attribute.setReplace(true);

                request.getAttribute().add(attribute);

            }

        }


        PutAttributesResponse response = sdb.putAttributes(request);

                    JOptionPane.showMessageDialog(SimpleDB.this,"Create Attributes Completed. ");

                } catch (Exception ex) {

                    JOptionPane.showMessageDialog(SimpleDB.this,"Error Executing Create Attributes. " + ex.getMessage());

                }

            }

        }
```

This method sets the domain name and the item name desired into the request. And also adds the non empty attributes entered in the Attributes jtable. Look at the delete attributes event handler shown below.

Delete Attributes event handler code

```
private class DeleteAttributes extends AbstractAction {

        private DeleteAttributes() {

            // JFormDesigner - Action initialization - DO NOT MODIFY    //GEN-BEGIN:initComponents
```

```java
// Generated using JFormDesigner Evaluation license - Aditya Yadav
putValue(NAME, "Delete Attributes");
// JFormDesigner - End of action initialization  //GEN-END:initComponents
}


public void actionPerformed(ActionEvent e) {
    try {
        AmazonSimpleDBClient sdb = AmazonClientFactory.getInstance().getSimpleDBClient();

        DeleteAttributesRequest request = new DeleteAttributesRequest();
        request.setItemName(textFieldItemName.getText());
        request.setDomainName(textFieldDomainName.getText());
        for (int i=0; i<tableAttributes.getModel().getRowCount();i++)
        {
            String name = (String)tableAttributes.getModel().getValueAt(i,0);
            String value = (String)tableAttributes.getModel().getValueAt(i,1);
            if (!name.trim().equals("") || !value.trim().equals("")){
                Attribute attribute = new Attribute();
                attribute.setName(name);
                attribute.setValue(value);
                request.getAttribute().add(attribute);
            }
        }
```

```
            DeleteAttributesResponse response = sdb.deleteAttributes(request);

                        JOptionPane.showMessageDialog(SimpleDB.this,"Delete Attributes Completed. ");

                        } catch (Exception ex) {

                                JOptionPane.showMessageDialog(SimpleDB.this,"Error Executing Delete Attributes. " + ex.getMessage());

                        }

                }

        }
```

The delete attributes event handler works just like the create attributes event handler it sets the domain name and item name, and the attributes from the Attributes jtable and fires a delete attributes request. Look at the get attributes event handler shown below.

Get Attributes event handler code

```
private class GetAttributes extends AbstractAction {

        private GetAttributes() {

                // JFormDesigner - Action initialization - DO NOT MODIFY    //GEN-BEGIN:initComponents

                // Generated using JFormDesigner Evaluation license - Aditya Yadav

                putValue(NAME, "Get Attributes");

                // JFormDesigner - End of action initialization  //GEN-END:initComponents

        }
```

```java
public void actionPerformed(ActionEvent e) {
    try {
        AmazonSimpleDBClient sdb = AmazonClientFactory.getInstance().getSimpleDBClient();

        GetAttributesRequest request = new GetAttributesRequest();
        request.setItemName(textFieldItemName.getText());
        request.setDomainName(textFieldDomainName.getText());
        GetAttributesResponse response = sdb.getAttributes(request);
        Object[] columnIdentifiers = new Object[]{"Name","Value"};

        ArrayList data = new ArrayList();
        int count=0;
        for (Attribute attribute : response.getGetAttributesResult().getAttribute())
        {
            data.add(new Object[]{attribute.getName(), attribute.getValue()});
            count++;
        }
        for (int i=count;count<100;count++) data.add(new Object[]{"",""});

        DefaultTableModel tableModel = (DefaultTableModel) tableAttributes.getModel();
        tableModel.setDataVector((Object[][]) data.toArray(new
```

```
Object[0][0]), columnIdentifiers);

                    JOptionPane.showMessageDialog(SimpleDB.this, "Get Attributes
Completed. ");

                } catch (Exception ex) {

                    JOptionPane.showMessageDialog(SimpleDB.this, "Error Executing
Get Attributes. " + ex.getMessage());

                }

            }

        }
```

The above code sets the domain name and the item name in the request and loops over the name/value(s) returned and updates the Attributes jtable. We are all done lets build the project and try it out in the next section.

Using the SimpleDB Manager

Enter 'mydomain' as domain name and hit create. And then click Commands->List Domain Names. See below. The domain will get created.

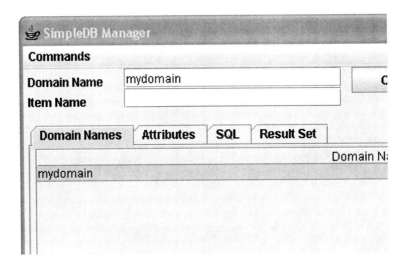

Figure 84 - Creating a SimpleDB Domain

Enter 'Aditya' as the item name. Click Attributes tab and enter City/Bangalore & Country/India as shown below. And hit Commands->Create Attributes.

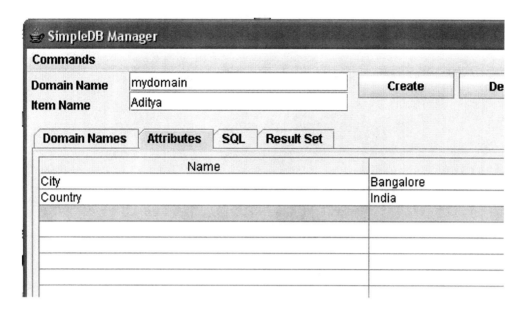

Figure 85 - Creating Attributes

On the AQL tab enter 'Select * from mydomain' and click Commands->Run SQL Query. And switch to ResultSet tab. As shown. The query will get executed and results displayed.

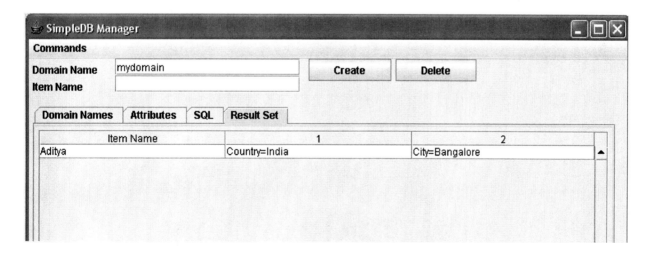

Figure 86 - Executing an SQL Query

Now hit the delete button. This will delete the domain. If you hit Commands->List Domain Names you will get a blank list.

Retrospective

We created a SimpleDB Manager and saw how SimpleDB allows Items to be stored in domains with arbitrary attributes. And we queried SimpleDB using an SQL like syntax.

Chapter 10- Relational Database Service

RDS is a fully relational database implemented over MySQL with patches to enable it to run on the AWS cloud infrastructure without many administration tasks. You can use regular MySQL tools without modification with the RDS instances. You can dynamically scale your database in terms of compute power and storage capacity up and down at anytime. AWS provides automatic backup of all RDS instances. RDS is very easy to setup in minutes and is accessible from an internet endpoint, and can be secured using AWS security groups and conventional mysql security features.

We are going to look at an RDS Manager application which will allow us to create, delete and list databases. The finished application looks as shown below

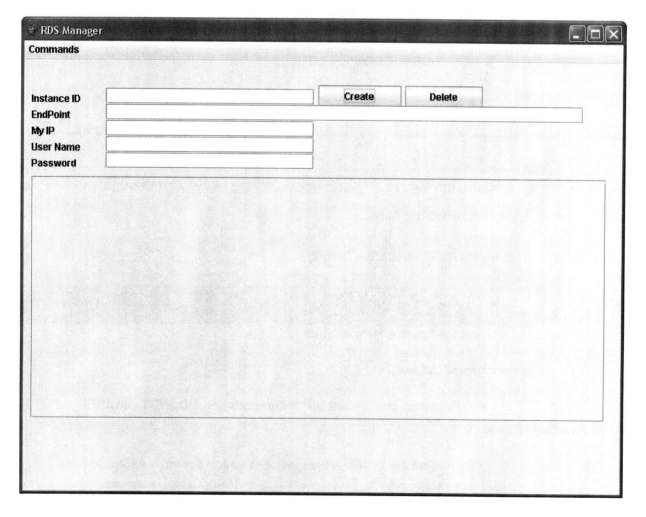

Figure 87 - The Finished RDS Manager Application

The menu has List Instances, Enable Access and Exit menu items. There is an instances list jtable at the bottom of the form. Let's look at the constructor.

RDS Manager constructor code

```
public RDSManager() {
        initComponents();

        this.setDefaultCloseOperation(JFrame.DO_NOTHING_ON_CLOSE);

        tableInstances.getSelectionModel().addListSelectionListener(new ListSelectionListener(){
                public void valueChanged(ListSelectionEvent e) {
                        try {
                                if (!e.getValueIsAdjusting()){
                                        String instanceID = (String) tableInstances.getValueAt(tableInstances.getSelectedRow(),0);
                                        textFieldInstanceID.setText(instanceID);
                                        String endpoint = (String) tableInstances.getValueAt(tableInstances.getSelectedRow(),1);
                                        textFieldEndpoint.setText(endpoint);
                                }
                        } catch (Exception ex){};
                }
        });
}
```

The constructor updates the instance id and endpoint text fields with the values from the selected row in the instances list jtable.

Look at the create event handler shown below.

Create event handler code

```
private class CreateInstance extends AbstractAction {

        private CreateInstance() {

                // JFormDesigner - Action initialization - DO NOT MODIFY   //GEN-BEGIN:initComponents

                // Generated using JFormDesigner Evaluation license - Aditya Yadav

                putValue(NAME, "Create");
```

// JFormDesigner - End of action initialization //GEN-END:initComponents
}

```java
public void actionPerformed(ActionEvent e) {
    try
    {
        AmazonRDSClient rds = AmazonClientFactory.getInstance().getRDSClient();

        CreateDBInstanceRequest request = new CreateDBInstanceRequest();

        request.setDBInstanceIdentifier(textFieldInstanceID.getText());

        request.setDBInstanceClass("db.m1.small");

        request.setAllocatedStorage(50);

        request.setDBName(textFieldInstanceID.getText());

        request.getDBSecurityGroups().add("default");

        request.setEngine("MySQL5.1");

        request.setBackupRetentionPeriod(3);

        request.setMasterUsername(textFieldUserName.getText());

        request.setMasterUserPassword(textFieldPassword.getText());


        CreateDBInstanceResponse response = rds.createDBInstance(request);

        JOptionPane.showMessageDialog(RDSManager.this,"Create Instance Completed. ");
```

```
            }
            catch (Exception ex)
            {
                JOptionPane.showMessageDialog(RDSManager.this,"Error    Executing    Create
Instance. " + ex.getMessage());
            }
        }
    }
}
```

This method creates a database. It makes a request with the instance id, small db machine size (RDS runs on top of EC2), 50 MB storage, the db name as the instance id, set default security group, engine to mysql 5.1 and the db username and db password. Look at the list instances method shown below.

List Instances event handler code

```java
private class ListInstances extends AbstractAction {

    private ListInstances() {

        // JFormDesigner - Action initialization - DO NOT MODIFY   //GEN-BEGIN:initComponents

        // Generated using JFormDesigner Evaluation license - Aditya Yadav

        putValue(NAME, "List Instances");

        // JFormDesigner - End of action initialization  //GEN-END:initComponents

    }



    public void actionPerformed(ActionEvent e) {
```

```java
            try
            {
                AmazonRDSClient rds = AmazonClientFactory.getInstance().getRDSClient();

                DescribeDBInstancesRequest request = new DescribeDBInstancesRequest();
                DescribeDBInstancesResponse response = rds.describeDBInstances(request);
                Object[] columnIdentifiers = new Object[]{"Instance ID", "Endpoint", "Status"};
                ArrayList data = new ArrayList();
                for(DBInstance instance : response.getDescribeDBInstancesResult().getDBInstance())
                {
                    data.add(new Object[]{instance.getDBInstanceIdentifier(), (instance.getEndpoint() == null?"":instance.getEndpoint().getAddress() + ":" + instance.getEndpoint().getPort()),instance.getDBInstanceStatus() });
                }
                DefaultTableModel tableModel = (DefaultTableModel)tableInstances.getModel();
                tableModel.setDataVector((Object[][])data.toArray(new Object[0][0]), columnIdentifiers);
                JOptionPane.showMessageDialog(RDSManager.this,"List Instances Completed. ");
            }
            catch (Exception ex)
            {
                JOptionPane.showMessageDialog(RDSManager.this,"Error Executing List Instances. " + ex.getMessage());
```

```
            }
        }
    }
```

This method makes a describe db instances request and populates Instance Id, Endpoint and Status into the JTable for each db instance. Look at the delete event handler code shown below.

Delete event handler code

```
private class DeleteInstance extends AbstractAction {

    private DeleteInstance() {

        // JFormDesigner - Action initialization - DO NOT MODIFY  //GEN-BEGIN:initComponents

        // Generated using JFormDesigner Evaluation license - Aditya Yadav

        putValue(NAME, "Delete");

        // JFormDesigner - End of action initialization  //GEN-END:initComponents

    }


    public void actionPerformed(ActionEvent e) {

        try
        {

            AmazonRDSClient rds = AmazonClientFactory.getInstance().getRDSClient();

            DeleteDBInstanceRequest request = new
```

```
DeleteDBInstanceRequest();

    request.setDBInstanceIdentifier(textFieldInstanceID.getText());

    request.setSkipFinalSnapshot(true);


    DeleteDBInstanceResponse response = rds.deleteDBInstance(request);

        JOptionPane.showMessageDialog(RDSManager.this,"Delete Instance Completed. ");

    }

    catch (Exception ex)

    {

        JOptionPane.showMessageDialog(RDSManager.this,"Error Executing Delete Instance. " + ex.getMessage());

    }

    }

}
```

This method makes a delete db request with the Instance ID and sets SkipFinalSnapshot to true, which means no snapshot will be taken before destroying the db and you will lose everything in that db. Look at the Enable Access method shown below.

Enable Access event handler code

```
private class EnableAccess extends AbstractAction {

    private EnableAccess() {

        // JFormDesigner - Action initialization - DO NOT MODIFY  //GEN-BEGIN:initComponents
```

```java
// Generated using JFormDesigner Evaluation license - Aditya Yadav
putValue(NAME, "Enable Access");
// JFormDesigner - End of action initialization  //GEN-END:initComponents
}


public void actionPerformed(ActionEvent e) {
    try
    {
        AmazonRDSClient rds = AmazonClientFactory.getInstance().getRDSClient();

        AuthorizeDBSecurityGroupIngressRequest request = new AuthorizeDBSecurityGroupIngressRequest();
        request.setDBSecurityGroupName("default");
        request.setCIDRIP(textFieldMyIP.getText()+"/32");

        AuthorizeDBSecurityGroupIngressResponse response = rds.authorizeDBSecurityGroupIngress(request);
        JOptionPane.showMessageDialog(RDSManager.this,"Enable Access Completed. ");
    }
    catch (Exception ex)
    {
        JOptionPane.showMessageDialog(RDSManager.this,"Error Executing Enable Access. " + ex.getMessage());
    }
```

```
        }
    }
```

This method enables access from your local desktop to the remote db by making an entry into the default security group for your ip address. We are all done lets build the project and run it in the next section.

Using RDS Manager

Think of and enter an Instance ID, I'm using 'mydb', set username to 'myuser' and password to 'mypassword'. Click Create button. And then click Commands->List Instances. See below.

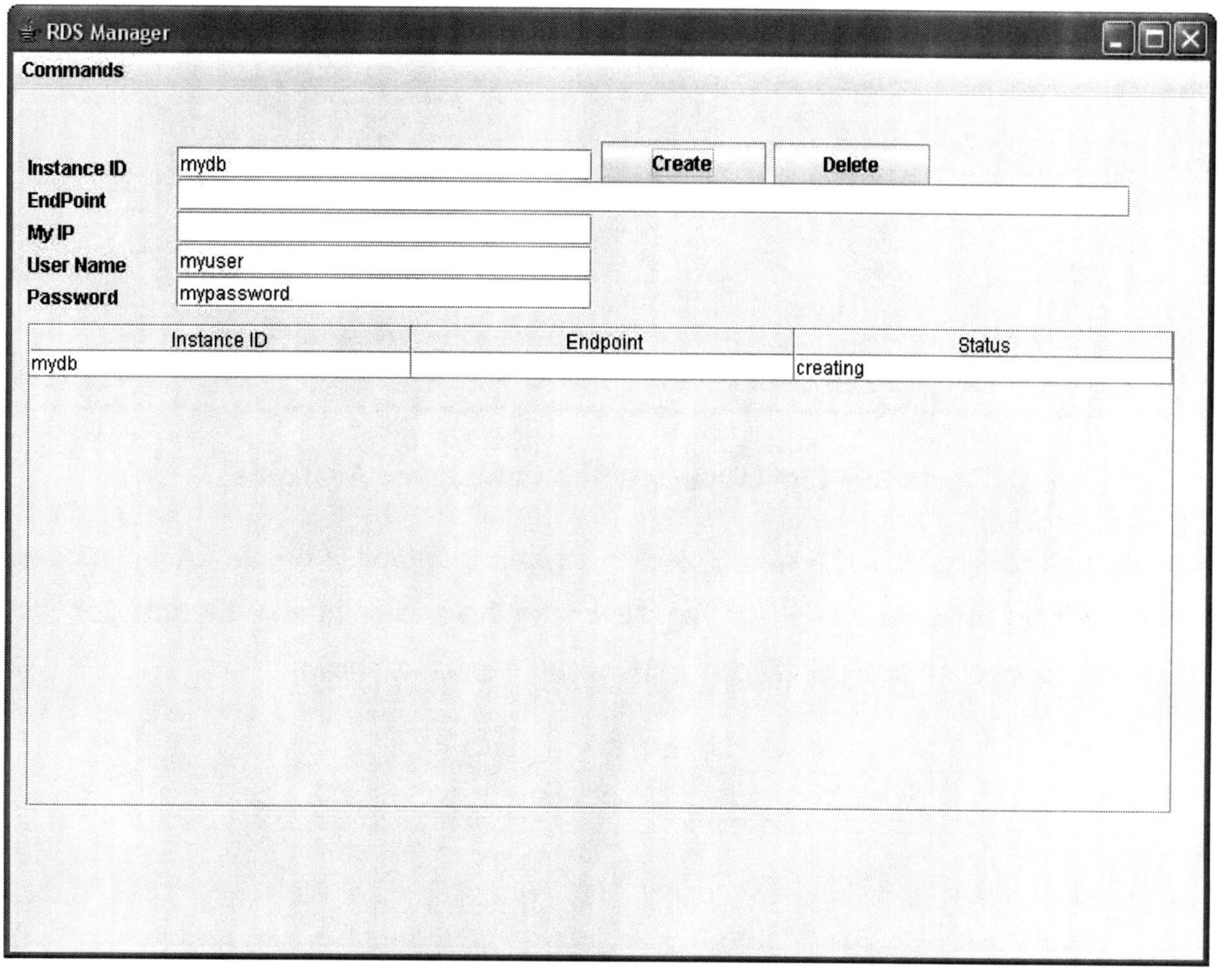

Figure 88 - Creating an RDS Instance

Wait for 2-5 minutes and keep hitting Commands->List Instances every minute. When the db is ready select it in the list view. Goto http://whatismyip.com and find your ip address and enter it in the My IP textbox and hit Commands->Enable Access. See below.

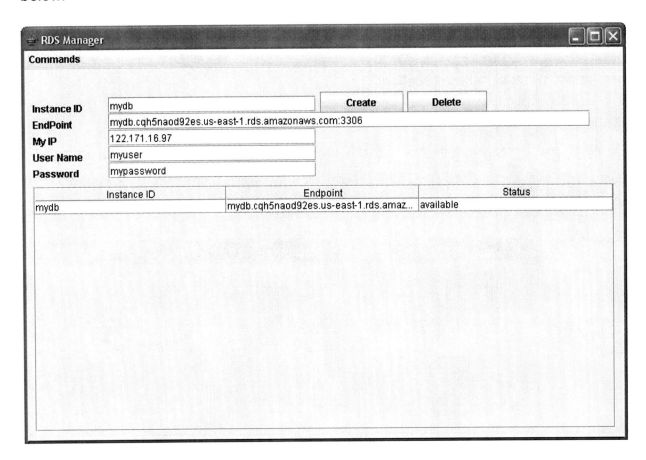

Figure 89 - List Instances Shows Instance Available

Now we can connect to it like we connect to any other database on our LAN. I'm using MYSQL Admin software called SQLyog. Now take the end point from the text box and create the connection configuration in your favourite tools as shown.

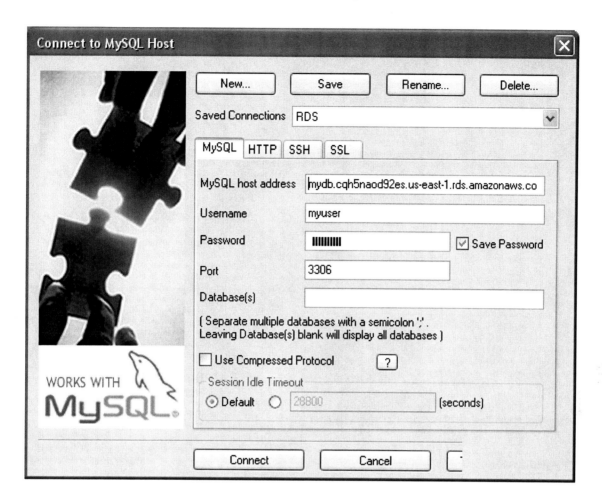

Figure 90 - Connecting To the RDS MySQL Instance Using Regular MySQL Tools

Hit connect. Now you have full access to the database. See Below.

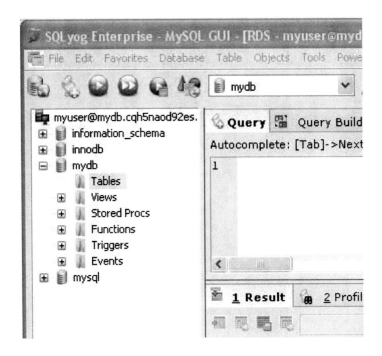

Figure 91 - Complete Access to RDS MySQL Instance

Now delete the db by clicking on the delete button in the RDS Manager.

Retrospective

We saw that RDS is actually a MySQL server that is patched for transparent scalability utilizing the Amazon infrastructure. We also saw that we can use our regular MySQL tools, drivers and API's to utilize RDS.

Chapter 11- Cloud Front

CloudFront is a web service to enable you to deliver content using AWS Edge servers spread through the globe with low latency and very high bandwidth. Of late it is also offering flash media streaming. It works off S3 buckets which store the files you want to deliver which is termed as the origin server. Every distribution sends the files to Edge Servers which serve the files from location nearest to the users, and cache the content for repeated delivery. Every time a CloudFront Distribution is updated it takes 10-20 minutes to spread out globally. You can assign custom domain names to the distributions so that they appear consistent with the rest of your web application assets.

We are going to create a command line application to list, provision and deprovision distributions. CloudFront is the API that allows you to expose the objects you store in a bucket to be distributed using Amazon's Edge servers distributed around the globe. Cloud Front is a Content Delivery Network (CDN).

Let's look at the constants and variable the program uses.

```
Constants and variable declarations
    private static final String COMMAND = "-command";
    private static final String LIST_VALUE = "list";
    private static final String PROVISION_VALUE = "provision";
    private static final String DEPROVISION_VALUE = "deprovision";
    private static final String BUCKET_COMMAND = "-bucket";
    private static final String ID_COMMAND = "-id";

    private static HashMap parameters = new HashMap();
```

We have declared constants for the commands we are going to read from the command line. The parameters HashMap is going to store the command line commands and values. Next let's see the PrintUsage method. If an exception is thrown in the program the exception message will be displayed and Usage will be printed.

printUsage method code

```
static void printUsage()
  {
    System.out.println("Usage:");
    System.out.println("Option 1: java -classpath <classpath> com.ayny.application.CloudFront -command:list");
    System.out.println("Option 2: java -classpath <classpath> com.ayny.application.CloudFront -command:provision -bucket:<bucketname>");
    System.out.println("Option 3: java -classpath <classpath> com.ayny.application.CloudFront -command:deprovision -id:<id>");
  }
```

As we see there are 3 use cases. First is used to list all the distributions in a CloudFront account. The second creates/provisions a distribution which serves files from the given bucket. And the third option is to deprovision/delete a distribution with the given id.

Let's see the method to parse the command line parameters as shown below.

parseParameters method

```
static void parseParameters(String[] args)
  {
    for (String arg : args)
    {
      int colonIndex = arg.indexOf(":");
      String command = arg.substring(0, colonIndex);
      String value = arg.substring(colonIndex+1);
      parameters.put(command, value);
      System.out.println("Command = "+command+" : value = "+value);
    }
  }
```

The command line parameters passed to this program will have the form - <command>:<value> so this method locates the colon and gets the command and value and stores then in the parameters HashMap. So a command line parameter like – command:list will be stored as parameters.Add("-command","list");

Now let's look at the main method.

main method

```java
public static void main(String[] args) throws Exception{
            try
    {
        parseParameters(args);
        String command = (String) parameters.get(COMMAND);
        if (command.equals(LIST_VALUE))
        {
           doList();
        }
        else if (command.equals(PROVISION_VALUE))
        {
           doProvision();
        }
        else if (command.equals(DEPROVISION_VALUE))
        {
           doDeprovision();
        }
        else
        {
           throw new Exception("Unrecognised command");
        }
    }
    catch (Exception ex)
    {
       System.out.println("Exception " + ex.getMessage());
       printUsage();
    }
      }
```

The main method first calls the parseParameters() method which parses and stores the Command and Value's in parameters HashMap. Then there are chained if else statements for the three use cases or list, provision and deprovision which call doList(), doProvision(), and doDeprovision() respectively. There is a try-catch block surrounding everything. In case an exception is thrown anywhere the exception message is printed on the console and the usage is printed.

Let's see the doList method.

doList method

```java
private static void doList() throws Exception
  {
        CloudFrontService cfs = AmazonClientFactory.getInstance().getCloudFrontService();
```

```
        Distribution[] distributions = cfs.listDistributions();
        for (Distribution distribution: distributions)
        {
            System.out.println("ID: "+distribution.getId()+" Domain: "+distribution.getDomainName() +
" Status: "+distribution.getStatus());
        }
        System.out.println("List Command Completed");
    }
```

This method iterates through the distributions in the result of a ListDistributions call. And prints the id, domain and status of the distribution. The domain will be used to access the files from the distribution as we will see a bit later,

Let's see the doProvision method.

doProvision method

```
private static void doProvision() throws Exception
    {
        CloudFrontService cfs = AmazonClientFactory.getInstance().getCloudFrontService();
        Distribution distribution = cfs.createDistribution((String)parameters.get(BUCKET_COMMAND));
        System.out.println("The ID to use while deleting: "+distribution.getId());
        System.out.println("Distribution Provisioned");
    }
```

This method makes a CreateDistribution request and passes the name of the bucket. This will create a distribution that is ready to serve files(objects) from the bucket. Finally this method will print the ID of the provisioned distribution which we will need to identify it in the list and to delete it later.

Let's create the doDeprovision method as follows.

doDeprovision method

```
private static void doDeprovision() throws Exception
    {
            CloudFrontService cfs = AmazonClientFactory.getInstance().getCloudFrontService();
        cfs.disableDistributionForDeletion((String)parameters.get(ID_COMMAND));
```

```
        System.out.println("It should take upto around 15 minutes!");
        while (true)
        {
            // need to pause a bit
            Thread.sleep(60000);

            try
            {
                cfs.deleteDistribution((String)parameters.get(ID_COMMAND));
                System.out.println("Distribution Deprovisioned");
                return;
            }
            catch (Exception e) { System.out.println("Patience Is a Virtue!"); }
        }
    }
```

This method makes a request to disable a distribution so that it can then be deleted next. Only a disabled distribution can be deleted and it can take upto 15 minutes to completely disable a distribution. Hence the next loop which tries to delete the distribution every 1 minute and only exits when it is successful and an exception is not thrown during its attempts (which is thrown if the distribution is not yet disabled and you try to delete it).

Using the CloudFront console application

We are all set. Use the S3 Manager to create a bucket and put a small file object in it. Also make the bucket public. Let's build the program and take it for a spin. We have created a bucket called 'adicloud'. R'ber to make the bucket public, otherwise CloudFront will not be able to serve objects from it.

Create a runtime configuration in eclipse which launches CloudFront.java as an application with the program arguments as '-command:provision -bucket:adicloud'. Run the configuration.

Creating a Distribution

```
...
2010-01-05 14:52:08,515 [main] DEBUG org.apache.commons.httpclient.HttpMethodBase - Resorting to protocol version default close connection policy
2010-01-05 14:52:08,515 [main] DEBUG org.apache.commons.httpclient.HttpMethodBase - Should NOT close connection, using HTTP/1.1
```

```
2010-01-05 14:52:08,515 [main] DEBUG org.apache.commons.httpclient.HttpConnection -
Releasing connection back to connection manager.
2010-01-05 14:52:08,515 [main] DEBUG
org.apache.commons.httpclient.MultiThreadedHttpConnectionManager - Freeing connection,
hostConfig=HostConfiguration[host=https://cloudfront.amazonaws.com]
2010-01-05 14:52:08,515 [main] DEBUG
org.apache.commons.httpclient.util.IdleConnectionHandler - Adding connection at:
1262683328515
2010-01-05 14:52:08,515 [main] DEBUG
org.apache.commons.httpclient.MultiThreadedHttpConnectionManager - Notifying no-one, there
are no waiting threads
The ID to use while deleting: E378K12WRUSTRK
Distribution Provisioned
```

The ID is E378K12WRUSTRK now let's list all distributions in our account. Create a runtime configuration in eclipse to launch CloudFront.java as an application with the program arguments '-command:list'

Listing Distributions

```
...

2010-01-05 14:54:39,796 [main] DEBUG org.apache.commons.httpclient.HttpMethodBase - Should
NOT close connection, using HTTP/1.1
2010-01-05 14:54:39,796 [main] DEBUG org.apache.commons.httpclient.HttpConnection -
Releasing connection back to connection manager.
2010-01-05 14:54:39,796 [main] DEBUG
org.apache.commons.httpclient.MultiThreadedHttpConnectionManager - Freeing connection,
hostConfig=HostConfiguration[host=https://cloudfront.amazonaws.com]
2010-01-05 14:54:39,796 [main] DEBUG
org.apache.commons.httpclient.util.IdleConnectionHandler - Adding connection at:
1262683479796
2010-01-05 14:54:39,796 [main] DEBUG
org.apache.commons.httpclient.MultiThreadedHttpConnectionManager - Notifying no-one, there
are no waiting threads
ID: E378K12WRUSTRK Domain: d2pvu6ghar7qlh.cloudfront.net Status: InProgress
List Command Completed
```

The domain for the distribution is d2pvu6ghar7qlh.cloudfront.net lets hit http://d2pvu6ghar7qlh.cloudfront.net/<myobjectkey> after a couple of minutes and the object/file will get downloaded. You have to try http://<domain>/<objectkey> with your own values.

Now let's deprovision the distribution. Please create a run configuration in eclipse that launches CloudFront.java as an application with the program arguments '-command:deprovision -id:E378K12WRUSTRK'. You have to put your distribution id which you got when you provisioned the distribution in the previous but one step. Deprovisioning can actually take upto 15 minutes, please be patient.

Deprovisioning a Distribution

```
...

2010-01-05 15:06:06,359 [main] DEBUG org.apache.commons.httpclient.HttpMethodBase -
Resorting to protocol version default close connection policy
2010-01-05 15:06:06,359 [main] DEBUG org.apache.commons.httpclient.HttpMethodBase - Should
NOT close connection, using HTTP/1.1
2010-01-05 15:06:06,359 [main] DEBUG org.apache.commons.httpclient.HttpConnection -
Releasing connection back to connection manager.
2010-01-05 15:06:06,359 [main] DEBUG
org.apache.commons.httpclient.MultiThreadedHttpConnectionManager - Freeing connection,
hostConfig=HostConfiguration[host=https://cloudfront.amazonaws.com]
2010-01-05 15:06:06,359 [main] DEBUG
org.apache.commons.httpclient.util.IdleConnectionHandler - Adding connection at:
1262684166359
2010-01-05 15:06:06,359 [main] DEBUG
org.apache.commons.httpclient.MultiThreadedHttpConnectionManager - Notifying no-one, there
are no waiting threads
Distribution Deprovisioned
```

Phew! It actually took just 7 minutes. The distribution has been deprovisioned, please go ahead and delete the objects in the bucket and then the bucket if you don't plan to use them anymore. They will incur a recurring charge small but nevertheless.

Retrospective

We learnt about CloudFront which is a CDN service provided by AWS which fits in with the other AWS offerings like S3. It can be used to deliver static files worldwide with low latency for our web applications. CloudFront also provides Flash Media Streaming (Just Announced) and BitTorrent protocols. Which is left for the readers to followup on.

Chapter 12- Simple Queue Service

SQS is a distributed queue system that delivers messages reliably from a producing component to a consuming component. The queue can deliver messages with any format limited to 8KB message sizes, for larger messages it is recommended that you store the message in S3 and pass the S3 metadata in the queue so that the consumer can access the actual payload directly from S3 and delete it when done along with deleting the message from the queue. SQS doesn't guarantee order of messages (not FIFO) usually that's not a problem but in case it is then messages should carry a custom sequence field put by the producer for use by the consumer. SQS locks the message while it is being processed and the consumer usually deletes the message using a key it received while receiving the message. No other consumer will be able to process the same message during this time. This eliminates the implicit possibility of multiple parallel recepients. If that needs to be implemented then a proxy consumer has to put identical copies of messages into all queues for each specific consumer.

SQS automatically purges messages which have been in the queue for 4 days. Every message has a visibility period which starts the moment the consumer receives the message and the consumer has to process and delete the message from the queue before the visibility period timesout otherwise the message will become available to other consumers.

We are going to see a small mail application (SQS Mail) using the SQS API's. We will be able to create and delete queues, list queues, send and receive messages.

See below to see what the application looks like when finished. You are not able to see the Send Message and Receive Message tab contents in the picture shown. They contain a textpane each. Let's look at the constructor code below. Each time the selection in the List Queues table changes it updates the Queue URL text field with the URL of the currently selected Queue.

The constructor code

```
public SQSMail() {
```

```java
            initComponents();
            this.setDefaultCloseOperation(JFrame.DO_NOTHING_ON_CLOSE);

            tableListQueues.getSelectionModel().addListSelectionListener(new ListSelectionListener(){
                public void valueChanged(ListSelectionEvent e) {
                    try {
                        if (!e.getValueIsAdjusting()){
                            String value = (String) tableListQueues.getValueAt(tableListQueues.getSelectedRow(),0);
                            textFieldQueueURL.setText(value);
                        }
                    } catch (Exception ex){};
                }
            });
        }
```

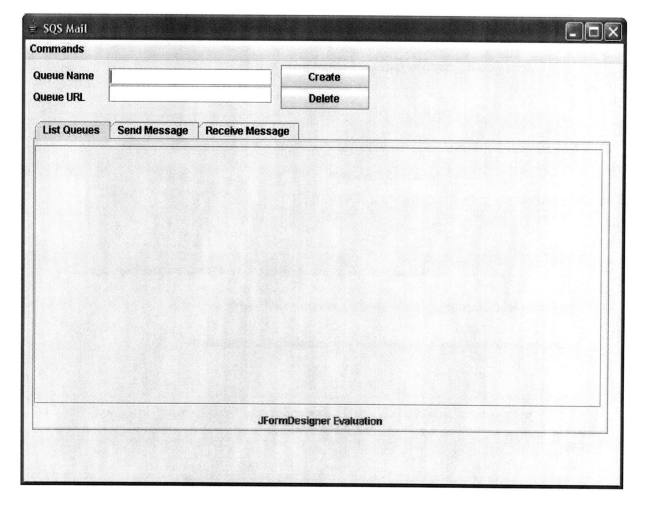

Figure 92 - Finished SQS Mail Application

Lets see the create queue event handler code.

Create Queue event handler code

```java
private class CreateQueue extends AbstractAction {

    private CreateQueue() {

        // JFormDesigner - Action initialization - DO NOT MODIFY    //GEN-BEGIN:initComponents
        // Generated using JFormDesigner Evaluation license - Aditya Yadav
        putValue(NAME, "Create");
        // JFormDesigner - End of action initialization  //GEN-END:initComponents
    }


    public void actionPerformed(ActionEvent e) {
        try
        {
            AmazonSQSClient sqs = AmazonClientFactory.getInstance().getSQSClient();


            CreateQueueRequest request = new CreateQueueRequest();

            request.setQueueName(textFieldQueueName.getText());

            CreateQueueResponse response = sqs.createQueue(request);


            JOptionPane.showMessageDialog(SQSMail.this,"Create Queue Completed. ");

        }
        catch (Exception ex)
```

```
            {
                JOptionPane.showMessageDialog(SQSMail.this,"Error Executing Create Queue. " + ex.getMessage());
            }
        }
    }
```

This method make's a create queue request with the queue name and shows a confirmation message popup. Let's see the event handler for delete queue.

Delete Queue event handler code

```
private class DeleteQueue extends AbstractAction {
        private DeleteQueue() {
            // JFormDesigner - Action initialization - DO NOT MODIFY  //GEN-BEGIN:initComponents
            // Generated using JFormDesigner Evaluation license - Aditya Yadav
            putValue(NAME, "Delete");
            // JFormDesigner - End of action initialization  //GEN-END:initComponents
        }



        public void actionPerformed(ActionEvent e) {
            try
            {
                AmazonSQSClient sqs = AmazonClientFactory.getInstance().getSQSClient();
```

```
                    DeleteQueueRequest request = new DeleteQueueRequest();

        request.setQueueUrl(textFieldQueueURL.getText());

        DeleteQueueResponse response = sqs.deleteQueue(request);



            JOptionPane.showMessageDialog(SQSMail.this,"Delete Queue Completed. ");

        }

        catch (Exception ex)

        {

            JOptionPane.showMessageDialog(SQSMail.this,"Error Executing Delete Queue. " + ex.getMessage());

        }

        }

    }
```

This method makes a delete queue request with the queue URL. Let's see the list queue event handler.

List Queues event handler code

```
private class ListQueues extends AbstractAction {

        private ListQueues() {

            // JFormDesigner - Action initialization - DO NOT MODIFY     //GEN-BEGIN:initComponents

            // Generated using JFormDesigner Evaluation license - Aditya Yadav
```

```java
            putValue(NAME, "List Queues");
        // JFormDesigner - End of action initialization  //GEN-END:initComponents
    }

    public void actionPerformed(ActionEvent e) {
        try
        {
            AmazonSQSClient sqs = AmazonClientFactory.getInstance().getSQSClient();

            ListQueuesRequest request = new ListQueuesRequest();
            ListQueuesResponse response = sqs.listQueues(request);
            Object[] columnIdentifiers = new Object[]{"Queue URL"};

            ArrayList data = new ArrayList();
            for(String queueURL : response.getListQueuesResult().getQueueUrl())
            {
                data.add(new Object[]{queueURL});
            }
            DefaultTableModel tableModel = (DefaultTableModel)tableListQueues.getModel();
            tableModel.setDataVector((Object[][])data.toArray(new Object[0][0]), columnIdentifiers);
            JOptionPane.showMessageDialog(SQSMail.this,"List Queues Completed. ");
        }
        catch (Exception ex)
```

```
            {
                JOptionPane.showMessageDialog(SQSMail.this,"Error Executing List Queues. " + ex.getMessage());
            }
        }
    }
```

This method makes a list queues request and iterates through the result and adds the queue urls for each queue to the queue list jtable. Now let's see the Send Message event handler.

Send Message event handler code

```
private class SendMessage extends AbstractAction {

    private SendMessage() {

        // JFormDesigner - Action initialization - DO NOT MODIFY   //GEN-BEGIN:initComponents

        // Generated using JFormDesigner Evaluation license - Aditya Yadav

        putValue(NAME, "Send Message");

        // JFormDesigner - End of action initialization  //GEN-END:initComponents
    }


    public void actionPerformed(ActionEvent e) {
        try
        {
            AmazonSQSClient sqs =
```

```
AmazonClientFactory.getInstance().getSQSClient();

            SendMessageRequest request = new SendMessageRequest();
    request.setQueueUrl(textFieldQueueURL.getText());
    request.setMessageBody(textPaneSendMessage.getText());
    SendMessageResponse response = sqs.sendMessage(request);

        JOptionPane.showMessageDialog(SQSMail.this,"Send Message Completed. ");
    }
    catch (Exception ex)
    {
        JOptionPane.showMessageDialog(SQSMail.this,"Error Executing Send Message. " + ex.getMessage());
    }
    }
}
```

This method calls the send message API and passes the queue URL and the body of the message to it. Let's see the receive message event handler.

Receive Message event handler code

```
private class ReceiveMessage extends AbstractAction {
    private ReceiveMessage() {
        // JFormDesigner - Action initialization - DO NOT MODIFY   //GEN-BEGIN:initComponents
```

```java
// Generated using JFormDesigner Evaluation license - Aditya Yadav
    putValue(NAME, "Receive Message");
    // JFormDesigner - End of action initialization  //GEN-END:initComponents
}


public void actionPerformed(ActionEvent e) {
    try
    {
        AmazonSQSClient sqs = AmazonClientFactory.getInstance().getSQSClient();

        ReceiveMessageRequest request = new ReceiveMessageRequest();
        request.setQueueUrl(textFieldQueueURL.getText());
        request.setMaxNumberOfMessages(1);
        ReceiveMessageResponse response = sqs.receiveMessage(request);
        if (response.getReceiveMessageResult().getMessage().size() >= 1)
        {

textPaneReceiveMessage.setText(response.getReceiveMessageResult().getMessage().get(0).getBody());

            DeleteMessageRequest deleteRequest = new DeleteMessageRequest();
            deleteRequest.setQueueUrl(textFieldQueueURL.getText());

deleteRequest.setReceiptHandle(response.getReceiveMessageResult().getMessage().get(0).getRe
```

```
ceiptHandle());
			DeleteMessageResponse deleteResponse = sqs.deleteMessage(deleteRequest);
		}


		JOptionPane.showMessageDialog(SQSMail.this,"Receive Message Completed. ");
	}
	catch (Exception ex)
	{
		JOptionPane.showMessageDialog(SQSMail.this,"Error Executing Receive Message. " + ex.getMessage());
	}
		}
	}
}
```

This method calls the Receive Message API by passing the queue URL and max number of messages to retrieve as 1. If a message is received it shows the body text of the message in the textpane and then it deletes the message by passing the queue URL and the message receipt handle it received along with the message.

We are all set. Build the project and let's take it for a test drive in the next section.

Using the SQS Mail application

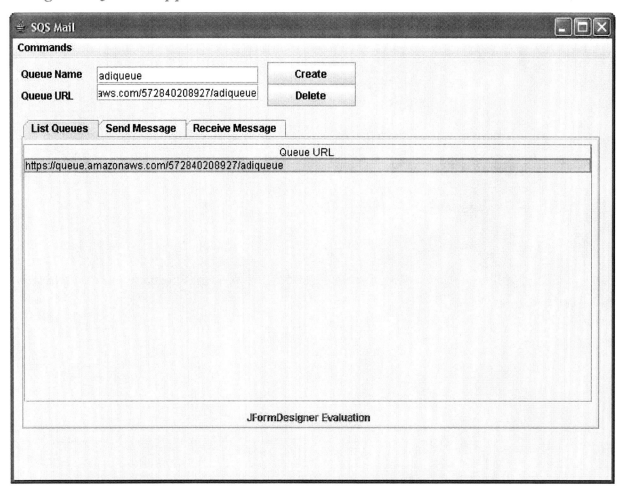

Figure 93 - Creating a Queue

Start the application and enter a queue name e.g. adiqueue and click create. You will get a confirmation. And then click the menu Commands->List Queues. The queue will show up in the list view. Select it with the mouse the queue URL will get copied into the queue URL text box. See above.

Select the Send Message tab and enter 'Hello World' in it and click Commands->Send Message menu. The message will get sent and you will get a confirmation. Now click Commands->Receive Message menu and goto the Receive Message tab. You will see the message will get received and the text showing in the text box. See below.

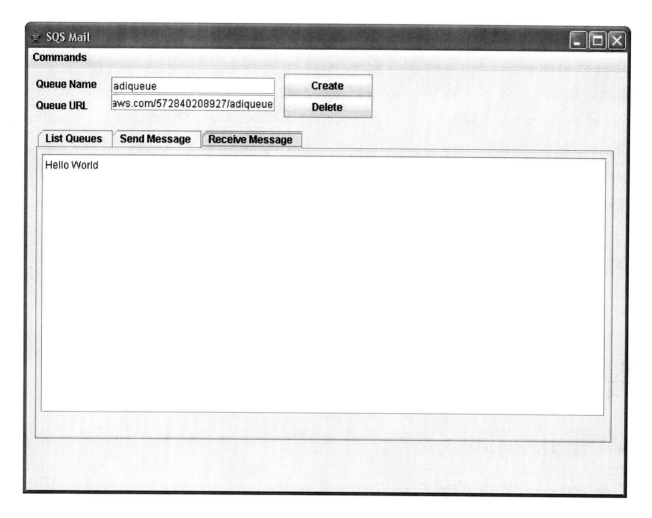

Figure 94 - Receiving a Message

Now click on the Delete button to delete the queue. And click Commands->List Queues a couple of times with a wait of 30 seconds each time. You will see that the queue has been removed.

Retrospective

We saw the Cloud version of Messaging systems we are used to, SQS. We created a simple Mail application to manage queues and send receive messages. We didn't try the concept of visibility in this chapter which is left to the reader to read up on.

Chapter 13- Elastic MapReduce

Elastic MapReduce is a service which allows easy processing of vast amounts of data stored in S3 using Hadoop running on preconfigured clustered Debian 5 EC2 instances. The Hadoop master node reads the data from S3, distributes data fragments and programs to multiple slave nodes which process the data fragments in parallel after which the master node combines the results and stores it back into S3.

We are going to run Map Reduce JobFlows on Amazon in this chapter. We have two console applications Mapper and Reducer with the following class contents. They are built and exported as JavaMapper.jar and JavaReducer.jar

Mapper source code

```java
package com.ayny;

import java.io.BufferedReader;

import java.io.InputStreamReader;

import java.util.StringTokenizer;


public class Mapper {

    public static void main(String[] args) throws Exception {

        BufferedReader br = new BufferedReader(new InputStreamReader(System.in));

        while (true){

            String line = br.readLine();

            if (line!=null){

                ProcessLine(line);
```

```
            } else {
                System.exit(0);
            }
        }
    }


    private static void ProcessLine(String line){
        StringTokenizer st = new StringTokenizer(line,".,;:\" []{}|-\t\r\n",false);
        while (st.hasMoreTokens()){
            String word = st.nextToken();
            System.out.println(word+"\t1");
            System.out.flush();
        }
    }

}
```

The mapper takes a text file. (Two files input1.txt and input2.txt are provided in the source code bundle) and goes over it line by line. For each word it encounters it prints the word then a tab and then '1'.

We are making a word count application. Go through the Reducer code.

Reducer source code

package com.ayny;

```java
import java.io.BufferedReader;

import java.io.InputStreamReader;

import java.util.HashMap;

import java.util.StringTokenizer;


public class Reducer {

    private static HashMap results = new HashMap();

    public static void main(String[] args) throws Exception {

        BufferedReader br = new BufferedReader(new InputStreamReader(System.in));

        while (true){

            String line = br.readLine();

            //System.out.println("Reducing:"+line);

            if (line!=null){

                ProcessLine(line);

            } else {

                for(Object w: results.keySet()){

                    System.out.println(((String)w)+"\t"+((Integer)results.get(w)).intValue());

                }

                System.exit(0);

            }
```

```
        }
    }


        private static void ProcessLine(String line){

            if (line.indexOf('\t')!= -1){

                String word = line.substring(0,line.indexOf('\t'));

                if (results.keySet().contains(word)){

                    int count = ((Integer) results.get(word)).intValue();

                    count++;

                    results.put(word,new Integer(count));


                }else {

                    results.put(word,new Integer(1));

                }

            }

        }


}
```

The Reducer takes the output from the Mapper and prints out a word then tab and then the count of its occurrences in the Mapper output. Build the projects export them as JavaMapper.jar and JavaReducer.jar and let's try them locally. Open a command prompt and goto the root folder of the workspace and type the following command. See Below.

Mapper Reducer local test run

G:\AdityaYadav.com\Books I'm writing\Amazon Cloud Computing With Java\workspace>

java -jar JavaMapper.jar <input1.txt | java -jar JavaReducer.jar

devoted 1

some   1

hate   2

focus   1

individuals   1

open   2

framework   1

as   1

standards   1

location   1

contributor   1

for   1

the   9

of   9

Bio   1

from   1

with   1

them   1

often   1

```
experience   1
you   2
leader  1
currently   1
Nitobi  1
this   1
mobile  2
about   1
core   1
Android 1
which   1
pain   1
2009   1
No   1
server  1
Java   1
user   1
having  1
more   1
…
```

Input1.txt is the input to the Mapper whos output is then piped to the Reducer. Amazon Elastic MapReduce works on predefined AMI's with Hadoop preinstalled. To execute the JobFlow both the mapper and reducer should have a definite end with a Zero exit code or else the job will fail. If the Mapper or Reducer runs for more than 10 minutes without any output then you have to print some comment text to the screen which is ignored by the next stage. To run arbitrary Mappers and Reducers in Python, Ruby, C++ etc. Hadoop provides a streaming method to run the JobFlow. In which both the mapper and reducers read from Standard Input and write to the Standard Output.

Somethings to note are to not use prepackaged mappers and reducers unless you know exactly how they function and fail or else debugging would be a nightmare. And also note the output bucket if is not empty the JobFlow will fail.

To Run a JobFlow you have to store the input files in an S3 bucket and designate a bucket to store the output, and the log (optional). You have to specify a Mapper and a Reducer and optionally cache files with the –cacheFile attribute. The Hadoop AMI on Amazon is based on Debian 5.0 and has ruby, python, java preinstalled. But not Mono (Mono is the .Net runtime for linux). Hopefully in future Amazon will preinstall mono on that image.

Open the S3 Manager and do the following-

1. Create a bucket with the name 'adimrinput'. And upload input1.txt and input2.txt with their filename as their keys.

2. Create a bucket with the name 'adimroutput'

3. Create a bucket with the name 'adilogoutput'

4. Create a bucket with the name 'adimrprog' and upload JavaMapper.jar and JavaReducer.jar into it with their filename as their keys.

See the configuration to run the MapReduce job we created above. The job flow name is not unique anything will do as long as you can identify your job flow. The type is streaming. Input location points to the adimrinput bucket which has our input files. The output is to be put in the adimroutput bucket which is emptied before every run. The mapper is 'java –jar JavaMapper.jar' and the reducer is 'java –jar JavaReducer.jar' but these files are not there on the running hadoop instance, to put them there we have to use the cachefile argument to load the file from the adimrprog bucket e.g. –cacheFile s3n://adimrprog/JavaMapper.jar#JavaMapper.jar which is used as 's3n://<bucketname>/<path to file>#<local path to file on the runtime where the file is put>'. We put both the JavaMapper.jar and the JavaReducer.jar using cacheFile args. We set the number of instances to 4 and the type of instance to m1.small. The log output goes to 'adilogoutput' bucket. And we choose a KeyPair to launch the instances with.

Upload the JavaMapper.jar and JavaReducer.jar into the 'adimrprog' bucket. Let's run the JobFlow through the Amazon Management Console.

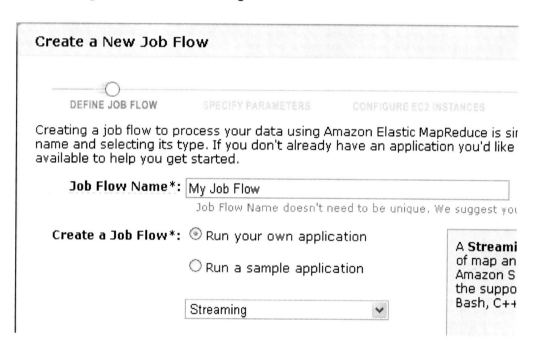

Figure 95 - Defining a New JobFlow

Select 'Run your own application' and choose 'Streaming'.

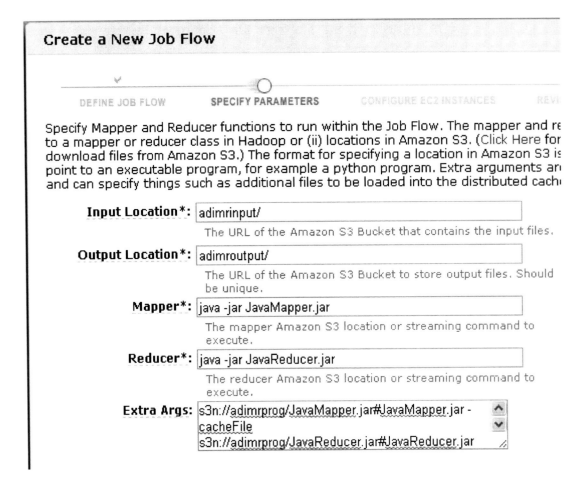

Figure 96 - Specifying the JobFlow Parameters

Specify the parameters as shown above.

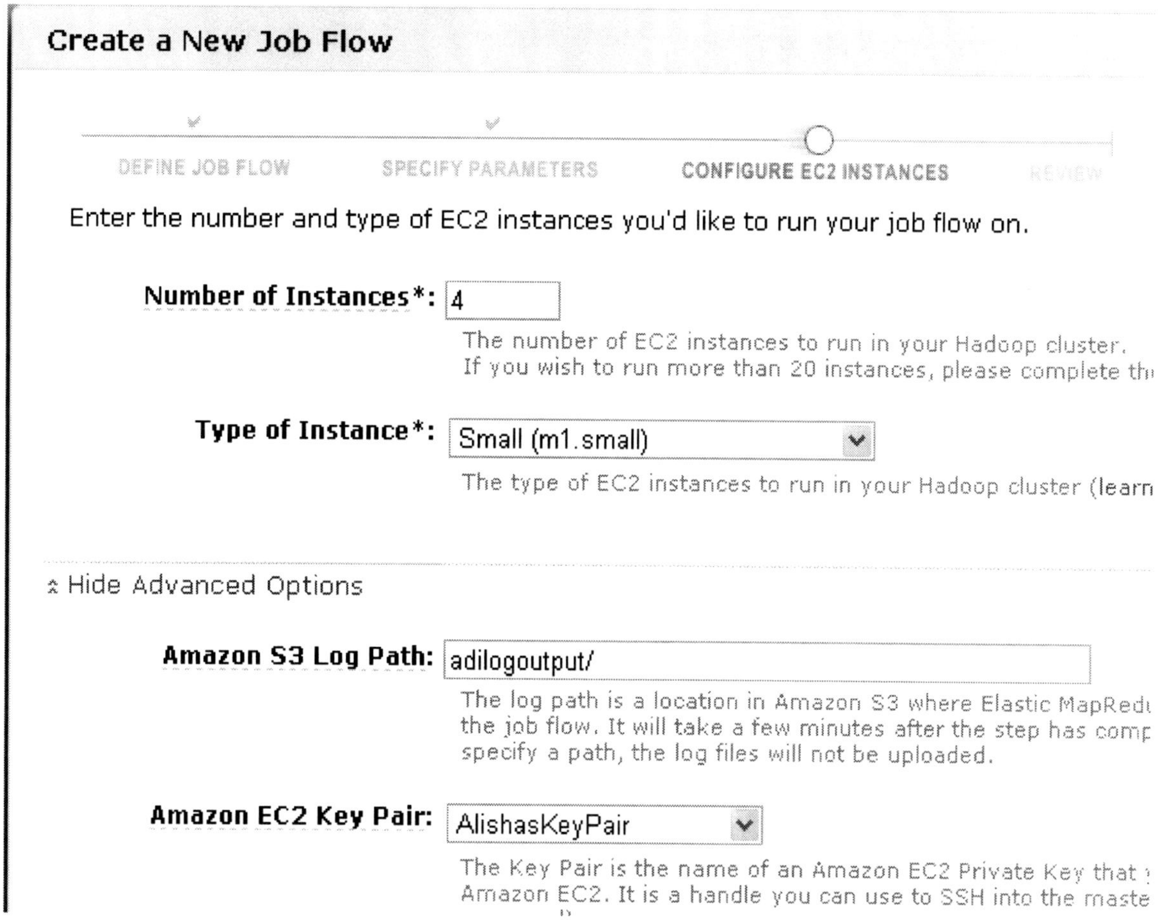

Figure 97 - Configuring EC2 Instances

Choose the KeyPair, Output log bucket, type of instance and number of instances.

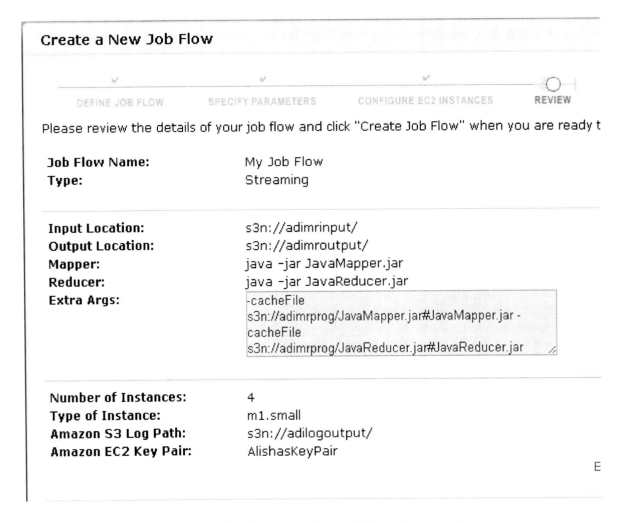

Figure 98 - Reviewing the JobFlow Parameters

Review the parameters and run the JobFlow.

Figure 99 - The JobFlow Starting

The JobFlow will take 10 minutes to complete. After it's completed it will show as shown below. You can retrieve the output from the 'adimroutput' bucket. Delete it to ready it for the next exercise.

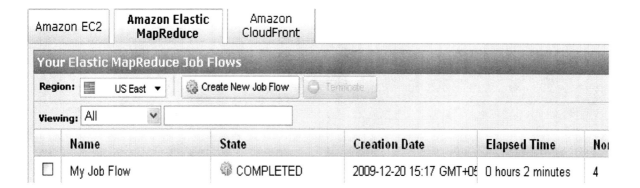

Figure 100 - The JobFlow Completed

Let's create a MapReduce Manager which will let us run JobFlows, which we can similarly use in our systems to run automated JobFlows.

The completed application looks as follows.

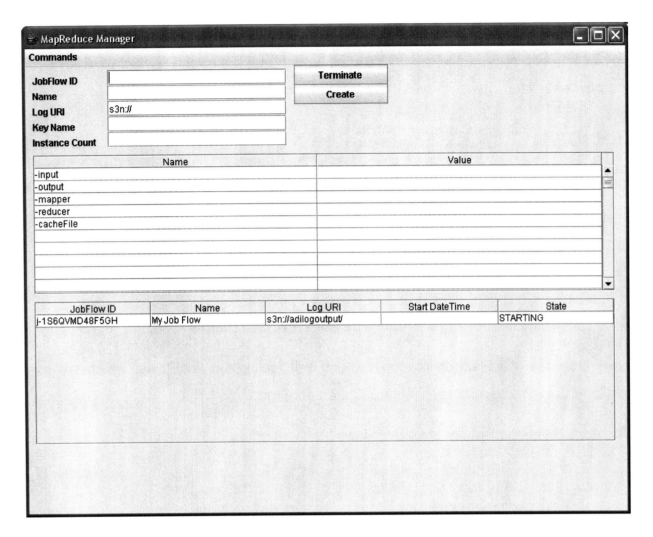

Figure 101 - The Finished MapReduce Manager Application

At the bottom is a jtable to list the job flows and above that is a jtable to enter the job flow parameters. The menu has one menu item 'List JobFlows'

Let's look at the constructor.

MapReduce Manager constructor code

```
public MapReduceManager() {
        initComponents();

        this.setDefaultCloseOperation(JFrame.DO_NOTHING_ON_CLOSE);

        tableJobFlows.getSelectionModel().addListSelectionListener(new
ListSelectionListener(){
                public void valueChanged(ListSelectionEvent e) {
                        try {
                                if (!e.getValueIsAdjusting()){
```

```
                              String jobFlowID = (String)
tableJobFlows.getValueAt(tableJobFlows.getSelectedRow(),0);
                              textFieldJobFlowID.setText(jobFlowID);
                         }
                    } catch (Exception ex){};
               }
          });
     }
```

The constructor has code to update the job flow id text field with the job flow id of the selected job in the jobflow list jtable everytime the selection is changed.

The list job flows event handler is as follows.

List JobFlows event handler code

```
public void actionPerformed(ActionEvent e) {
          try
     {
                    AmazonElasticMapReduceClient emr = AmazonClientFactory.getInstance().getElasticMapReduceClient();

                    DescribeJobFlowsRequest request = new DescribeJobFlowsRequest();
          DescribeJobFlowsResponse response = emr.describeJobFlows(request);
               Object[] columnIdentifiers = new Object[]{"JobFlow ID", "Name", "Log URI","Start DateTime","State"};
                    ArrayList data = new ArrayList();
               for(JobFlowDetail detail : response.getDescribeJobFlowsResult().getJobFlows())
               {
                 String startDateTime = "";
                 String state = "";
                 if (detail.getExecutionStatusDetail() != null){
                         if (detail.getExecutionStatusDetail().getStartDateTime() != null) startDateTime = detail.getExecutionStatusDetail().getStartDateTime();
                         if (detail.getExecutionStatusDetail().getState() != null) state = detail.getExecutionStatusDetail().getState();
                 }
                                   data.add(new Object[]{(detail.getJobFlowId()==null?"":detail.getJobFlowId()), (detail.getName()==null?"":detail.getName()), (detail.getLogUri()==null?"":detail.getLogUri()), startDateTime, state});
               }
               DefaultTableModel tableModel = (DefaultTableModel)tableJobFlows.getModel();
               tableModel.setDataVector((Object[][])data.toArray(new Object[0][0]), columnIdentifiers);
               JOptionPane.showMessageDialog(MapReduceManager.this,"List JobFlows Completed. ");
          }
          catch (Exception ex)
```

```
                {
                    JOptionPane.showMessageDialog(MapReduceManager.this,"Error Executing List
JobFlows. " + ex.getMessage());
                }
            }
```

The above code makes a list request and iterates through the results. It populates JobFlowId, Name, LogUri, StartDateTime and State into the jobflow list jtable. See the Create JobFlow event handler code.

Create JobFlow event handler code

```
private class CreateJobFlow extends AbstractAction {

    private CreateJobFlow() {

        // JFormDesigner - Action initialization - DO NOT MODIFY  //GEN-BEGIN:initComponents

        // Generated using JFormDesigner Evaluation license - Aditya Yadav

        putValue(NAME, "Create");

        // JFormDesigner - End of action initialization  //GEN-END:initComponents

    }


    public void actionPerformed(ActionEvent e) {

        try
        {
            AmazonElasticMapReduceClient    emr    = AmazonClientFactory.getInstance().getElasticMapReduceClient();


            RunJobFlowRequest request = new RunJobFlowRequest();
```

```java
request.setLogUri(textFieldLogURI.getText());

request.setName(textFieldName.getText());

JobFlowInstancesConfig config = new JobFlowInstancesConfig();

config.setEc2KeyName(textFieldKeyName.getText());

config.setInstanceCount(Integer.parseInt(textFieldInstanceCount.getText()));

config.setKeepJobFlowAliveWhenNoSteps(false);

config.setMasterInstanceType("m1.small");

config.setSlaveInstanceType("m1.small");

PlacementType pType = new PlacementType();

pType.setAvailabilityZone("us-east-1a");

config.setPlacement(pType);

request.setInstances(config);


StepConfig stepConfig = new StepConfig();

stepConfig.setName("Hadoop Streaming Step");

HadoopJarStepConfig jarStepConfig = new HadoopJarStepConfig();

jarStepConfig.setJar("/home/hadoop/contrib/streaming/hadoop-0.18-streaming.jar");

for (int i=0; i<tableStepParams.getModel().getRowCount(); i++)
{
    String name = (String)tableStepParams.getModel().getValueAt(i,0);

    String value = (String)tableStepParams.getModel().getValueAt(i,1);

    if (name != null && !name.trim().equals("") && value!=null && !value.trim().equals("")){

        jarStepConfig.getArgs().add(name);
```

```
                jarStepConfig.getArgs().add(value);

          }

      }

      stepConfig.setHadoopJarStep(jarStepConfig);

      request.getSteps().add(stepConfig);

      RunJobFlowResponse response = emr.runJobFlow(request);

              JOptionPane.showMessageDialog(MapReduceManager.this,"Create     JobFlow Completed. ");

      }

      catch (Exception ex)

      {

              JOptionPane.showMessageDialog(MapReduceManager.this,"Error     Executing Create JobFlow. " + ex.getMessage());

      }

          }

      }
```

The above code setsup the request with various parameters from the text boxes and hard codes a lot of others. It reads the arguments from the parameters jtable and runs a single step JobFlow.

The terminate jobflow event handler code is shown below.

Terminate JobFlow event handler code

```
private class TerminateJobFlow extends AbstractAction {

        private TerminateJobFlow() {
```

```java
            // JFormDesigner - Action initialization - DO NOT MODIFY   //GEN-BEGIN:initComponents
            // Generated using JFormDesigner Evaluation license - Aditya Yadav
            putValue(NAME, "Terminate");
            // JFormDesigner - End of action initialization   //GEN-END:initComponents
        }

        public void actionPerformed(ActionEvent e) {
            try
            {
                AmazonElasticMapReduceClient emr = AmazonClientFactory.getInstance().getElasticMapReduceClient();

                TerminateJobFlowsRequest request = new TerminateJobFlowsRequest();
                request.getJobFlowIds().add(textFieldJobFlowID.getText());
                TerminateJobFlowsResponse response = emr.terminateJobFlows(request);
                JOptionPane.showMessageDialog(MapReduceManager.this,"Terminate JobFlow Completed. ");
            }
            catch (Exception ex)
            {
                JOptionPane.showMessageDialog(MapReduceManager.this,"Error Executing Terminate JobFlow. " + ex.getMessage());
            }
```

```
            }
        }
```

The event handler makes a terminate JobFlow request with the JobFlow Id. We are all done lets build the application and take it for a test drive in the next section.

Using MapReduce Manager

Enter the values in the text boxes and grids as shown in the following picture, hit Create button and click Commands->List JobFlows

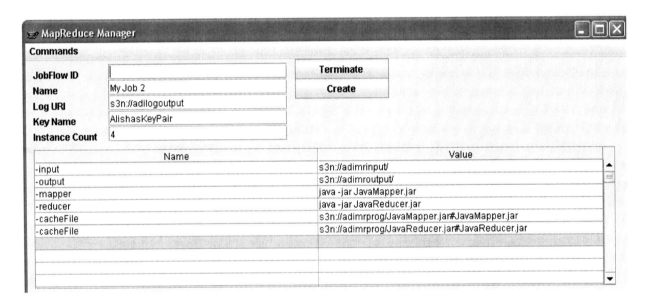

Figure 102 - Creating a JobFlow

The JobFlow takes about 10 minutes to complete. Click Commands->List JobFlows every minute to see the JobFlow Status. Once completed it will showup as follows in the MapReduce Manager and the AWS Console. And you can access the output from 'adimroutput' bucket and logs from 'adilogoutput' bucket.

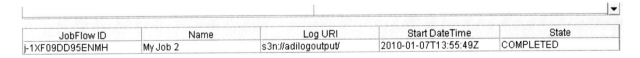

Figure 103 - JobFlow Completed

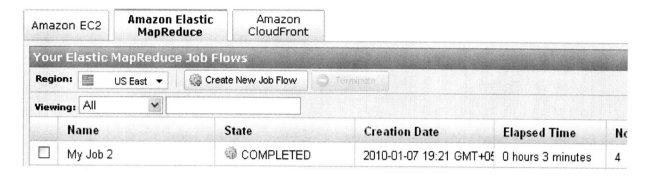

Figure 104 - The JobFlow Showing as Completed in AWS Console

Retrospective

We created Mapper and Reducer applications in Java and learnt that mono is not installed on the Debian 5 image Amazon uses for MapReduce. We tested the Mapper and Reducer locally using the command line with input output piping as a sanity check. We setup buckets with input and programs, and to receive output and log messages. R'ber if the output bucket is not empty the JobFlow would fail. We ran streaming JobFlows which could be used to run arbitrary programs as Mappers and Reducers. We ran a single step JobFlow, multistep JobFlows is left as an exercise to the reader. Also the reader should read about Hive and Pig which are also available on Elastic MapReduce.

Chapter 14- Agile Continuous Integration with Amazon EC2 using Ant

In this chapter we are going to develop a small web application with just the login page and hook it up with an Ant build file. We will be running functional tests with selenium on it. A common concern with agile teams is how cloud infrastructure fits in with their agile methodology and this chapter is dedicated to the Continuous Integration Agile (XP) practice. We will create Ant Tasks to deploy our web application onto a runtime instance which we will provision and we will run the functional tests on it, after which we will deprovision the running instance. The Ant build file can be configured in a CI Server like Teamcity and we can put the source code in a VCS, changes to which can trigger an automated build. We are going to stop at building the Ant script and tasks; the integration with a CI server is not covered and is left as an exercise to the user.

Let's start by looking at the Ant Tasks and the sample web application. Open index.jsp in the AWSToolkitDemo Web Application Project.

index.jsp code listing

```jsp
<?xml version="1.0" encoding="ISO-8859-1" ?>
<%@ page language="java" contentType="text/html; charset=ISO-8859-1"
    pageEncoding="ISO-8859-1"%>
<!DOCTYPE html PUBLIC "-//W3C//DTD XHTML 1.0 Transitional//EN"
"http://www.w3.org/TR/xhtml1/DTD/xhtml1-transitional.dtd">
<html xmlns="http://www.w3.org/1999/xhtml">
<head>
<meta http-equiv="Content-Type" content="text/html; charset=ISO-8859-1" />
<title>Insert title here</title>
</head>
<body>
<%
String status ="Failure";
if ((request.getParameter("login") !=null) && (request.getParameter("login").equals("guest")) &&
     (request.getParameter("password") !=null) &&
(request.getParameter("password").equals("guest"))){
     status="Success";
}
%>
<form id="myform" method="post">
<%=status %><br/>
Login: <input id="login" name="login" type="text" value="<%=request.getParameter("login") %>"/><br/>
```

```
Password: <input id="password" name="password" type="password"
value="<%=request.getParameter("password") %>"/><br/>
<input id="submitbutton" name="submitbutton" type="submit" value="Submit"/>
</form>

</body>
</html>
```

We have created a simple login form with login and password text boxes and a submit button. And we self submit to the same page where we check if both the login and password are equal to 'guest' in which case we display Success, otherwise Failure is displayed by default.

Let's run the Website to see how it works. We will deploy it locally on a local Tomcat 6 installation, we assume you know how to download and install tomcat server and create a local tomcat configuration. Right click on index.jsp->Run As->Run On Server and select the local tomcat instance.

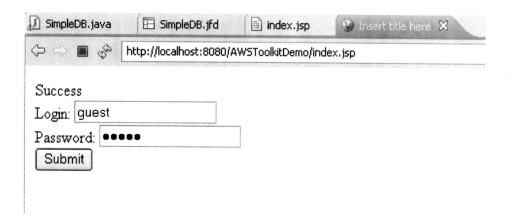

Figure 105 - Logging into the Web Application

Now download Firefox and Selenium from http://www.mozilla.com/en-US/firefox/firefox.html and http://seleniumhq.org/download/. Download the Selenium IDE and Selenium RC. IDE is used to record test cases and RC (Remote Control) plays them. Selenium IDE requires Firefox to work. Start Firefox and drop the 'selenium-ide-1.0.2.xpi' file you downloaded into its webpage space. Go ahead and install it. Extract the RC zip file. Download and install JDK 1.6 on the machine and put it on the system

PATH. See the batch file to start selenium server as shown below. We are using JDK 1.5 for the code we are writing but selenium requires JDK 1.6 so we are temporarily setting it up with JDK 1.6 in the script.

StartSeleniumServer.bat

```
Echo Selenium Server Requires JDK1.6 to be installed and on the PATH

@echo off

set JAVA_HOME=c:\jdk1.6

set PATH=%JAVA_HOME%\bin;%PATH%

java -jar "selenium-remote-control-1.0.1\selenium-server-1.0.1\selenium-server.jar"

Pause
```

Double click the batch file to start the selenium server. See Below.

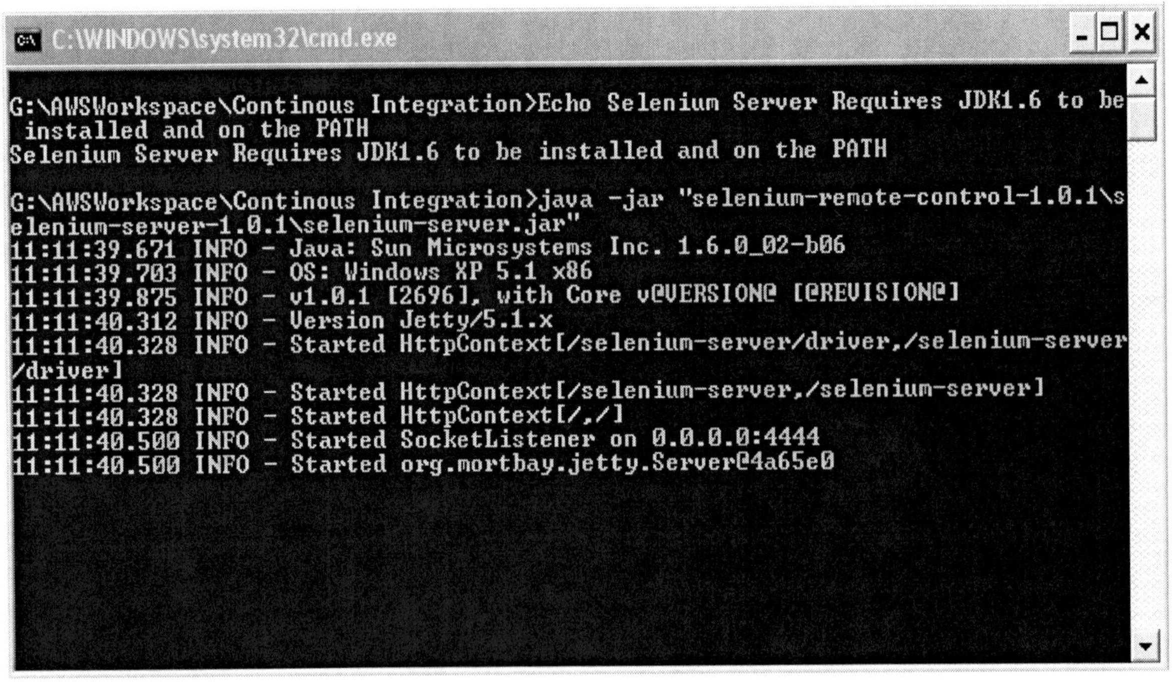

Figure 106 - Selenium Server Started

In Firefox click Tools->Selenium IDE. Enter http://localhost:8080 as the Base URL. Open http://localhost:8080/AWSToolkitDemo/index.jsp in Firefox. Hit the red round record button in selenium ide and go back to the login page, enter 'guest' as the login and password and hit submit. All this while Selenium IDE is recording it. See Below.

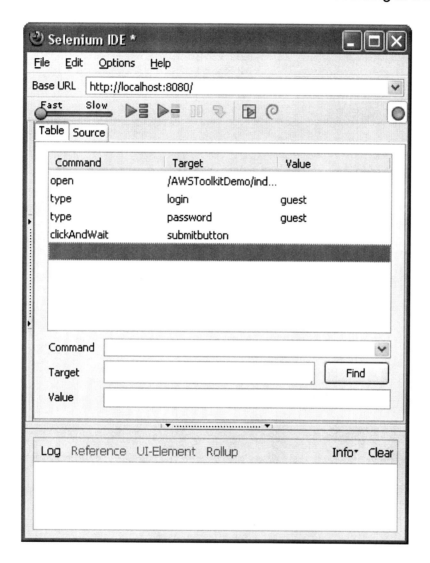

Figure 107 - Selenium IDE Recording a Test Case

Now we have to add an assert statement to the recording which will wait for the page to load after submit and check if Success has been displayed or not. Click the next line after clickAndWait and right click and select Insert New Command. Now select the line again and select assertTextPresent as the command. And value as 'Success' as shown below. Also put a setTimeout statement before the clickAndWait statement with 30000 as the value (this is in ms).

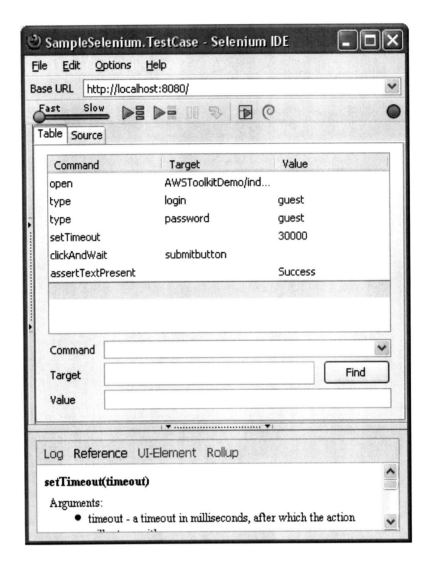

Figure 108 - Putting the Timeout & Assert Statements

Hit the play button with 3 green lines. Selenium will play the test in FireFox. See Below.

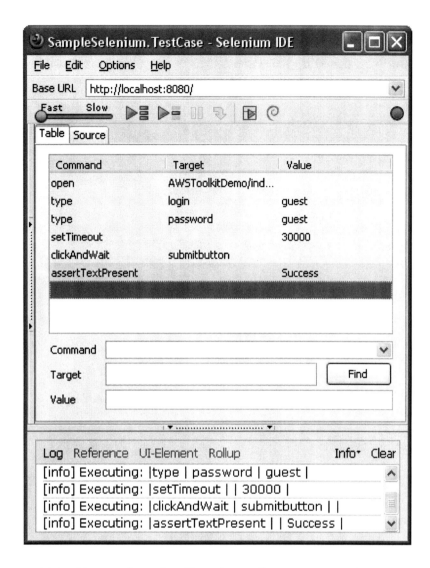

Figure 109 - Executing the TestCase From Within Selenium IDE

It shows that the assert statement has passed. Now let's save the test using File->Save Test Case as… And also export the test to JUnit test java file using "File->Export Test Case as->Java (Junit) Selenium RC" into a Tests folder in the workspace with the name SampleSeleniumTest.java in the package com.example.tests

Now let's prepare our Bundle and AMI on which our Ant (we will write it in a while) build script will run the tests on. We will choose a Windows 2003 server from the instance-store (S3) run it as an instance. Login into it through Remote Desktop and install an FTP server FileZilla on it. So that out Ant script can copy/ftp over the Website onto it. And we will also configure the Tomcat as a windows service to run the web application when it gets loaded through Ant.

Back to the Amazon console. Start an instance as shown below. I have chosen the 'ami-df20c3b2' ami. You could choose the same or another similar one.

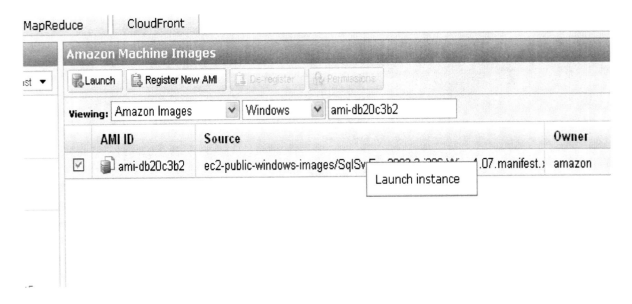

Figure 110 - Launching a Windows AMI

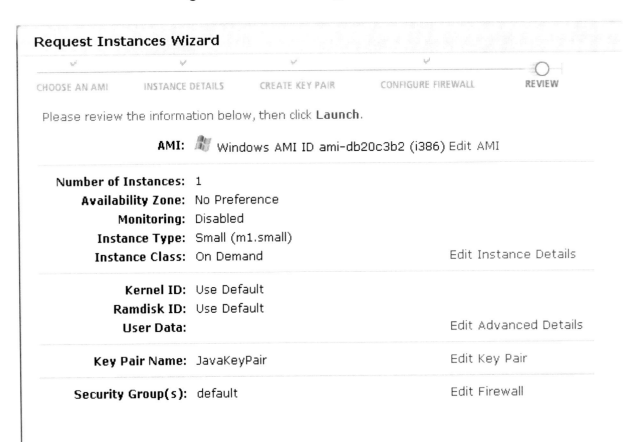

Figure 111 - Launch Instance Wizard

Add your ip into the default security group with both TCP/UDP ports 0-65535 and <my-ip>/32 as values. Get your ip address from http://whatismyip.com Make sure the machine is ready by looking at the System Log for the 'Windows is Read to use' message. Get the password to the machine and open a Remote Desktop Session to it.

Download and install JDK 1.5 on the machine. Also download tomcat 6 and install it on the machine. Install tomcat as service by executing 'service.bat install' from the command prompt in the tomcat\bin directory. Goto Start->All Programs->Administrative Tools->Services and make the Tomcat service startup type 'Automatic' and start it. Create the directory "C:\apache-tomcat-6.0.20\webapps\AWSToolkitDemo" we will ftp files into this directory.

Download Filezilla server from http://filezilla-project.org/download.php?type=server and install it on the machine and start the FileZilla server interface by clicking ok and leaving everything as default. You should set an admin password in a production system.

Click Edit->Users, General, Add. Set the name to 'ciaccount' and password to 'a63jhsd'. Select Shared Folders->Add and select the 'C:\apache-tomcat-6.0.20\webapps\AWSToolkitDemo' folder. Click Set as Home, and select all the File and Directory permissions. On your desktop machine start an ftp client and upload the contents of the 'AWSToolkitDemo\WebContent\' web application project contents we saw earlier to the FTP Server on the running instance.

Hit http://localhost:8080/AWSToolkitDemo/index.jsp on the running instance. You should be able to see the login page. You can go back to Selenium IDE and run the test on this website by changing the base URL to http://<ServerPublicDNS>:8080/

If you want a new password to be generated each time an instance is launched from your bundled image you can change the setting in %ProgramFiles%\Amazon\Ec2ConfigSetup\config.xml and change the state of

Ec2SetPassword to enabled. Otherwise you have store the password to this instance safely and all instances launched from its bundle will have the same password.

We are all set to now build a bundle and register an ami. In S3 Manager Tool provided with this book enter a unique bucket name and click Put Bucket. R'ber the bucket name you use. On the Amazon console create a bundle out of the running instance with the same bucket name. When the bundling is over register an AMI with the bundle. Note down the AMI Image id we will need it while making the Ant file.

Please download the Source code for this book from the author's website. We are going to walk through the essential portions of it. Please refer to the source code.

Ant build.xml file

```xml
<project name="ContinousIntegrationFunctionalTestingBuild" default="run" basedir=".">
    <property name="build.dir" value="build"/>
      <property name="lib.dir" value="AWSManager/lib"/>
      <property name="webapp.dir" value="AWSToolkitDemo/WebContent"/>
      <property name="src.tests" value="Tests"/>

    <path id="everything">
        <fileset dir="${lib.dir}" includes="**/*.jar"/>
          <fileset dir="." includes="AntPlugin.jar"/>
          <pathelement path="${build.dir}"/>
          <filelist dir="${build.dir}" files="**/*.class"/>
          <fileset dir="selenium-remote-control-1.0.1\selenium-java-client-driver-1.0.1" includes="selenium-java-client-driver.jar"/>
    </path>

    <taskdef resource="AMIAntTask.properties" classpathref="everything"/>
    <taskdef resource="net/sf/antcontrib/antcontrib.properties">
      <classpath>
        <pathelement location="ant-contrib-0.6.jar"/>
      </classpath>
    </taskdef>

   <target name="provisionamiinstance" description="Provision AMI Instance">
      <provisionamitask amazonkey="" secretkey="" amiimageid="" keyPairName="" texttocheckfor="Windows is Ready"></provisionamitask>
        <loadfile srcfile="dns.txt" property="dns" failonerror="true"/>
        <ftp server="${dns}" userid="ciaccount" password="a63jhsd" action="put" remotedir="/" port="21" passive="no" binary="yes"> <!--connectmode="ACTIVE">-->
          <fileset dir="${webapp.dir}" includes="**/*.*"/>
        </ftp>
```

```xml
    </target>

    <target name="runfunctionaltests" description="Runs the functional tests using selenium RC">
        <delete dir="${build.dir}"/>
        <mkdir dir="${build.dir}"/>
        <javac srcdir="${src.tests}" destdir="${build.dir}">
            <classpath refid="everything"/>
        </javac>
        <junit printsummary="yes" haltonfailure="yes" showoutput="true">
          <classpath refid="everything"/>
          <formatter type="plain"/>
            <batchtest fork="true">
                    <fileset dir="${build.dir}" includes="**/*.class" />
            </batchtest>
        </junit>
    </target>

    <target name="deprovisionamiinstance" description="Deprovision AMI Instance">
        <deprovisionamitask amazonkey="" secretkey="" ></deprovisionamitask>
    </target>


    <target name="run">
       <trycatch>
            <try>
                <antcall target="provisionamiinstance" inheritall="true" inheritrefs="true"/>
                <antcall target="runfunctionaltests" inheritall="true" inheritrefs="true"/>
            </try>
            <finally>
                <antcall target="deprovisionamiinstance" inheritall="true" inheritrefs="true"/>
            </finally>
       </trycatch>
    </target>
</project>
```

The project has a default target of 'run' which will do everything. We define the dns property. It will be used to read from the dns.txt file and will store the dns which the ftp task will use to transfer files to the running instance. We have created a path with the name 'everything' which contains all the classes and jars we have in the project.

The next things are the taskdef. We are loading the Ant contrib tasks (try/catch/finally task), our own task(s) which we have made (shown later). The provisionamiinstance target calls our provisionamitask which will run an instance based on the ami-image-id we provide, and then will wait for it to start and be ready, then get its instanceid and dns and write it to instanceid.txt and dns.txt files respectively. The target then reads the dns from dns.txt file into dns property. Then the ftp task connects to the server at this dns and transfers our webapp to it.

The runfunctionaltests task does what it says. It compiles all the tests in the Tests folder and runs them. In our sample test Selenium is being driven to run functional test(s) on the website running on the remote instance. The deprovisionamiinstance target calls the deprovisionamitask which will terminate the instance we are using for testing. The run target is the main target which runs and has a try finally block. It calls provisionamiinstance and runfunctionaltests targets and will finally call deprovisionamiinstance. Which means irrespective of our build failing or succeeding the running instance will be deprovisioned. Enter amazonKey, secretKey, and the Ami ID and keyPairName values relevant for your settings.

We have modified the Sample Test. Please refer to the listing below.

SampleSeleniumTest.java code listing

```java
package com.example.tests;

import com.thoughtworks.selenium.*;

import java.util.regex.Pattern;

import java.io.File;

import java.io.FileInputStream;

import java.io.FileOutputStream;


public class SampleSeleniumTest extends SeleneseTestCase {
```

```java
    public void setUp() throws Exception {

        String dns = readFromFile("dns.txt");

        setUp("http://"+dns+":8080/", "*chrome");

    }



    public void testSampleSelenium() throws Exception {

        selenium.open("AWSToolkitDemo/index.jsp");

        selenium.type("login", "guest");

        selenium.type("password", "guest");

        selenium.setTimeout("");

        selenium.click("submitbutton");

        selenium.waitForPageToLoad("30000");

        assertTrue(selenium.isTextPresent("Success"));

    }



    public static String readFromFile(String filename) throws Exception
    {

        File file = new File(filename);

        FileInputStream fis = new FileInputStream(file);

        byte[] data = new byte[(int)file.length()];

    fis.read(data);

    fis.close();

    return new String(data);
```

```
    }
}
```

We have added a method to read a line from a file. And we use that to read the dns from dns.txt which belongs to the running instance and is stored in the file by the provisionamitask which we have written (shown later). We use this dns to point selenium to the right base URL.

Let's go back to the AntPlugin project and look at three class files and one properties file with the names ContinousIntegrationDestroyAMITask.java, ContinousIntegrationStartAMITask.java, Utility.java, and AMIAntTask.properties. See the listings for the same below and their explanations.

ContinousIntegrationStartAMITask

```java
package com.ayny.ant.task;

import org.apache.tools.ant.Task;
import org.apache.tools.ant.Project;

public class ContinuousIntegrationStartAMITask extends Task {

    private String instanceID;
    private String amazonKey;
    private String secretKey;
    private String amiImageID;
    private String keyPairName;
```

```java
        private String textToCheckFor;


    public void execute() {

        try {

            Utility.runInstance(amazonKey, secretKey, amiImageID, keyPairName);

            instanceID = Utility.readFromFile("instanceid.txt");

            Utility.waitTillInstanceReady(amazonKey, secretKey, instanceID,

                    keyPairName, textToCheckFor);


        } catch (Exception ex) {

            System.out.println(ex.getMessage());

            ex.printStackTrace();

        }

    }



    public String getInstanceID() {

        return instanceID;

    }



    public void setInstanceID(String instanceID) {

        this.instanceID = instanceID;

    }
```

```java
        public String getAmazonKey() {

                return amazonKey;

        }


        public void setAmazonKey(String amazonKey) {

                this.amazonKey = amazonKey;

        }


        public String getSecretKey() {

                return secretKey;

        }


        public void setSecretKey(String secretKey) {

                this.secretKey = secretKey;

        }


        public String getAmiImageID() {

                return amiImageID;

        }


        public void setAmiImageID(String amiImageID) {

                this.amiImageID = amiImageID;

        }
```

```java
        public String getKeyPairName() {

            return keyPairName;

        }



        public void setKeyPairName(String keyPairName) {

            this.keyPairName = keyPairName;

        }



        public String getTextToCheckFor() {

            return textToCheckFor;

        }



        public void setTextToCheckFor(String textToCheckFor) {

            this.textToCheckFor = textToCheckFor;

        }

}
```

We have private variables to store the values and their getters and setters and an execute method which will get called through ant which will call RunInstance method and read the instanceid which it stores in the instanceid.txt file and then calls the WaitTillInstanceReady method.

ContinousIntegrationStopAMITask

```java
package com.ayny.ant.task;

import org.apache.tools.ant.Task;

import org.apache.tools.ant.Project;


public class ContinousIntegrationStopAMITask  extends Task {


    private String instanceID;

    private String amazonKey;

    private String secretKey;


        public String getInstanceID() {

                return instanceID;

        }


        public void setInstanceID(String instanceID) {

                this.instanceID = instanceID;

        }


        public String getAmazonKey() {

                return amazonKey;

        }


        public void setAmazonKey(String amazonKey) {
```

```java
        this.amazonKey = amazonKey;
    }


    public String getSecretKey() {

        return secretKey;

    }


    public void setSecretKey(String secretKey) {

        this.secretKey = secretKey;

    }


    public void execute() {

        try {

            instanceID = Utility.readFromFile("instanceid.txt");

            Utility.terminateInstance(amazonKey, secretKey, instanceID);

        } catch (Exception e){

            System.out.println(e.getMessage());

            e.printStackTrace();

        }
    }


}
```

We have three private variables to store keys and instance id. With their getters and setters. And an execute method with reads the instanceid from instanceid.txt file and calls the Terminate instance method.

Utility.java

```java
package com.ayny.ant.task;

import java.io.File;

import java.io.FileInputStream;

import java.io.FileOutputStream;


import org.apache.commons.codec.binary.Base64;


import com.amazonaws.ec2.AmazonEC2;

import com.amazonaws.ec2.AmazonEC2Client;

import com.amazonaws.ec2.model.DescribeInstancesRequest;

import com.amazonaws.ec2.model.DescribeInstancesResponse;

import com.amazonaws.ec2.model.GetConsoleOutputRequest;

import com.amazonaws.ec2.model.GetConsoleOutputResponse;

import com.amazonaws.ec2.model.MonitoringSpecification;

import com.amazonaws.ec2.model.Reservation;

import com.amazonaws.ec2.model.RunInstancesRequest;

import com.amazonaws.ec2.model.RunInstancesResponse;

import com.amazonaws.ec2.model.RunningInstance;

import com.amazonaws.ec2.model.TerminateInstancesRequest;
```

```java
public class Utility {

    public static String readFromFile(String filename) throws Exception
    {
        File file = new File(filename);
        FileInputStream fis = new FileInputStream(file);
        byte[] data = new byte[(int)file.length()];
        fis.read(data);
        fis.close();
        return new String(data);
    }


    public static void writeToFile(String fileName, String text) throws Exception
    {
        FileOutputStream fos = new FileOutputStream(fileName);
        fos.write(text.getBytes());
        fos.close();
    }


    public static boolean isInstanceReady(String amazonKey, String secretKey, String instanceID, String keyPairName, String textToCheckFor) throws Exception
    {
        AmazonEC2 ec2 = new AmazonEC2Client(amazonKey,secretKey);
```

```java
        GetConsoleOutputRequest request = new GetConsoleOutputRequest();

        request.setInstanceId(readFromFile("instanceid.txt"));

        GetConsoleOutputResponse response = ec2.getConsoleOutput(request);

        if (response.getGetConsoleOutputResult().getConsoleOutput().getOutput() != null && !response.getGetConsoleOutputResult().getConsoleOutput().getOutput().trim().equals(""))

        {

            if (new String(Base64.decodeBase64(response.getGetConsoleOutputResult().getConsoleOutput().getOutput().getBytes())).contains(textToCheckFor)) return true;

            else return false;

        }

        else

        {

            return false;

        }

    }


    public static void waitTillInstanceReady(String amazonKey, String secretKey, String instanceID, String keyPairName, String textToCheckFor) throws Exception

    {

        while (true)

        {

            System.out.println("Checking if instance is ready");

            try{

                Thread.sleep(30000);
```

```java
            } catch (Exception ex){}
        if (isInstanceReady(amazonKey, secretKey, instanceID, keyPairName, textToCheckFor))
        {
         System.out.println("Instance Ready!!!");
            recoverDNS(amazonKey, secretKey, instanceID);
            return;
        }
    }
}


public static void runInstance(String amazonKey, String secretKey, String amiImageID, String keyPairName) throws Exception
{
        System.out.println("Running instance");
    AmazonEC2 ec2 = new AmazonEC2Client(amazonKey,secretKey);


    RunInstancesRequest request = new RunInstancesRequest();
    request.setImageId(amiImageID);
    request.setKeyName(keyPairName);
    request.setMinCount(1);
    request.setMaxCount(1);
    MonitoringSpecification spec = new MonitoringSpecification();
    spec.setEnabled(true);
    request.setMonitoring(spec);
```

```java
        request.getSecurityGroup().add("default");

        request.setInstanceType("m1.small");

        RunInstancesResponse response = ec2.runInstances(request);

writeToFile("instanceid.txt",response.getRunInstancesResult().getReservation().getRunningInstance().get(0).getInstanceId());

        System.out.println("Written instanceid to file");

    }


    public static void recoverDNS(String amazonKey, String secretKey, String instanceID) throws Exception
    {

        System.out.println("Recovering dns");

        AmazonEC2 ec2 = new AmazonEC2Client(amazonKey,secretKey);

        DescribeInstancesRequest request = new DescribeInstancesRequest();

        request.getInstanceId().add(instanceID);

        DescribeInstancesResponse response = ec2.describeInstances(request);

        Reservation reservation = response.getDescribeInstancesResult().getReservation().get(0);

        RunningInstance runningInstance = reservation.getRunningInstance().get(0);

        writeToFile("dns.txt", runningInstance.getPublicDnsName());

        writeToFile("build\\dns.txt", runningInstance.getPublicDnsName());

        System.out.println("Written dns to file");



    }
```

```java
    public static void terminateInstance(String amazonKey, String secretKey, String instanceID)
throws Exception
    {
        System.out.println("Terminating instance");

        AmazonEC2 ec2 = new AmazonEC2Client(amazonKey,secretKey);

        TerminateInstancesRequest request = new TerminateInstancesRequest();

        request.getInstanceId().add(instanceID);

        ec2.terminateInstances(request);

        System.out.println("Instance Terminated");

    }

}
```

The utility class powers the Ant Plugins (The Two Tasks) we have made. It has methods to Read/Write to file, check if instance is ready, wait till instance is ready, recover dns from a running instance, and terminate a running instance and to run an instance.

AMIAntTask.properties

```
deprovisionamitask=com.ayny.ant.task.ContinousIntegrationStopAMITask
provisionamitask=com.ayny.ant.task.ContinuousIntegrationStartAMITask
```

This properties file links the names with which the tasks are refered in the ant build.xml file and the classes which implement those tasks.

The output from the selenium server and the tail of the build script output is shown below.

Selenium Server Output
Echo Selenium Server Requires JDK1.6 to be installed and on the PATH **Selenium Server Requires JDK1.6 to be installed and on the PATH** 18:56:06.265 INFO - Java: Sun Microsystems Inc. 1.6.0_02-b06 18:56:06.265 INFO - OS: Windows XP 5.1 x86 18:56:06.265 INFO - v1.0.1 [2696], with Core v@VERSION@ [@REVISION@] 18:56:06.343 INFO - Version Jetty/5.1.x 18:56:06.343 INFO - Started HttpContext[/selenium-server/driver,/selenium-server/driver] 18:56:06.343 INFO - Started HttpContext[/selenium-server,/selenium-server] 18:56:06.343 INFO - Started HttpContext[/,/] 18:56:06.359 INFO - Started SocketListener on 0.0.0.0:4444 18:56:06.359 INFO - Started org.mortbay.jetty.Server@3a6727 19:15:19.187 INFO - Checking Resource aliases 19:15:19.187 INFO - Command request: getNewBrowserSession[*chrome, http://ec2-174-129-45-186.compute-1.amazonaws.com:8080/,] on session null 19:15:19.203 INFO - creating new remote session 19:15:19.328 INFO - Allocated session afd09adeff6545bfbca5bdd503704a08 for http://ec2-174-129-45-186.compute-1.amazonaws.com:8080/, launching... 19:15:19.500 INFO - Preparing Firefox profile... 19:15:21.890 INFO - Launching Firefox...

```
19:15:24.468 INFO - Got result: OK,afd09adeff6545bfbca5bdd503704a08 on session a
fd09adeff6545bfbca5bdd503704a08
19:15:24.468 INFO - Command request: open[AWSToolkitDemo/index.jsp, ] on session
 afd09adeff6545bfbca5bdd503704a08
19:15:27.078 INFO - Got result: OK on session afd09adeff6545bfbca5bdd503704a08
19:15:27.093 INFO - Command request: type[login, guest] on session afd09adeff654
5bfbca5bdd503704a08
19:15:27.109 INFO - Got result: OK on session afd09adeff6545bfbca5bdd503704a08
19:15:27.109 INFO - Command request: type[password, guest] on session afd09adeff
6545bfbca5bdd503704a08
19:15:27.125 INFO - Got result: OK on session afd09adeff6545bfbca5bdd503704a08
19:15:27.125 INFO - Command request: setTimeout[, ] on session afd09adeff6545bfb
ca5bdd503704a08
19:15:27.140 INFO - Got result: OK on session afd09adeff6545bfbca5bdd503704a08
19:15:27.156 INFO - Command request: click[submitbutton, ] on session afd09adeff
6545bfbca5bdd503704a08
19:15:27.171 INFO - Got result: OK on session afd09adeff6545bfbca5bdd503704a08
19:15:27.187 INFO - Command request: waitForPageToLoad[30000, ] on session afd09
adeff6545bfbca5bdd503704a08
19:15:27.812 INFO - Got result: OK on session afd09adeff6545bfbca5bdd503704a08
19:15:27.812 INFO - Command request: isTextPresent[Success, ] on session afd09ad
eff6545bfbca5bdd503704a08
19:15:27.843 INFO - Got result: OK,true on session afd09adeff6545bfbca5bdd503704
```

a08

19:15:27.843 INFO - Command request: testComplete[,] on session afd09adeff6545bfbca5bdd503704a08

19:15:27.843 INFO - Killing Firefox...

19:15:28.046 INFO - Got result: OK on session afd09adeff6545bfbca5bdd503704a08

Ant Build Output

...

[provisionamitask] Written dns to file

   [ftp] sending files

   [ftp] 3 files sent

runfunctionaltests:

  [delete] Deleting directory G:\AdityaYadav.com\Books I'm writing\Amazon Cloud Computing With Java\workspace\build

   [mkdir] Created dir: G:\AdityaYadav.com\Books I'm writing\Amazon Cloud Computing With Java\workspace\build

   [javac] Compiling 1 source file to G:\AdityaYadav.com\Books I'm writing\Amazon Cloud Computing With Java\workspace\build

   [junit] Running com.example.tests.SampleSeleniumTest

   [junit] Tests run: 1, Failures: 0, Errors: 0, Time elapsed: 8.953 sec

deprovisionamiinstance:

```
[deprovisionamitask] Terminating instance
[deprovisionamitask] 2010-01-12 19:15:30,031 [main] DEBUG org.apache.commons.htt
pclient.params.DefaultHttpParams - Set parameter http.useragent = Jakarta Common
s-HttpClient/3.1
[deprovisionamitask] 2010-01-12 19:15:30,031 [main] DEBUG org.apache.commons.htt
pclient.params.DefaultHttpParams - Set parameter http.protocol.version = HTTP/1.
1
...
 [deprovisionamitask] 2010-01-12 19:15:32,031 [main] DEBUG com.amazonaws.ec2.Amaz
onEC2Client - Attempting to transform TerminateInstancesResponse type...
[deprovisionamitask] 2010-01-12 19:15:32,250 [main] DEBUG com.amazonaws.ec2.Amaz
onEC2Client - Transformed response to: <?xml version="1.0" encoding="UTF-8"?>
[deprovisionamitask] <TerminateInstancesResponse xmlns="http://ec2.amazonaws.com
/doc/2009-11-30/">
[deprovisionamitask] <ResponseMetadata>
[deprovisionamitask] <RequestId>7a636633-da42-4b8c-8fcc-4bfff4a6b5a5</RequestId>

[deprovisionamitask] </ResponseMetadata>
[deprovisionamitask] <TerminateInstancesResult>
[deprovisionamitask] <TerminatingInstance>
[deprovisionamitask] <InstanceId>i-6274420a</InstanceId>
[deprovisionamitask] <CurrentState>
[deprovisionamitask] <Code>32</Code>
```

```
[deprovisionamitask] <Name>shutting-down</Name>

[deprovisionamitask] </CurrentState>

[deprovisionamitask] <PreviousState>

[deprovisionamitask] <Code>16</Code>

[deprovisionamitask] <Name>running</Name>

[deprovisionamitask] </PreviousState>

[deprovisionamitask] </TerminatingInstance>

[deprovisionamitask] </TerminateInstancesResult>

[deprovisionamitask] </TerminateInstancesResponse>

[deprovisionamitask]

[deprovisionamitask] 2010-01-12 19:15:32,250 [main] DEBUG com.amazonaws.ec2.AmazonEC2Client - Attempting to unmarshal into the TerminateInstancesResponse type..

...

[deprovisionamitask] 2010-01-12 19:15:32,281 [main] DEBUG com.amazonaws.ec2.AmazonEC2Client - Unmarshalled response into TerminateInstancesResponse type.

[deprovisionamitask] Instance Terminated


BUILD SUCCESSFUL

Total time: 19 minutes 23 seconds
```

Give it a spin. Double click StartBuild.bat file in the source code provided along with this book.

Retrospective

We created a small web app and deployed it on an Amazon AMI we prepared. We ran automated functional tests using Selenium IDE & RC triggered from the Ant build file. Implementing this in an actual development environment with a Version Control System and TeamCity or other CI Server is left as an exercise to the reader.

Chapter 15-Using Eclipse for AWS Development

In this chapter we are going to configure AWS Toolkit. We are then going to create a small web application. We will run the application locally and then we will run and debug it on AWS, followed by going through different views to manage ami's, elastic block storage, instances and security groups. We have already installed JDK1.5, eclipse and AWS toolkit in the Prepping chapter.

Configuring AWS Toolkit

Goto https://aws-portal.amazon.com/gp/aws/developer/account/index.html?ie=UTF8&action=access-key and get your account number, access key, secret key, create the X.509 certificate and download the certificate and its private key file and then goto https://console.aws.amazon.com/ec2/home#c=EC2&s=KeyPairs and create a key pair and download and store its key file.

Start eclipse and click Window->Preferences-AWS Toolkit and enter your account number, access key id, secret access key, select the certificate and its private key file. Click Apply.

Then click External Tools and browse and select the putt and puttygen executables. Click Apply. As shown in the picture.

Click Key Pairs. Your Key Pairs from the account will show up. But they don't have the private key files associated with them. Right click on the Key Pair you just created and plan to use for this chapter, and browse and select its key.

Click Regions and leave the default selected and click ok.

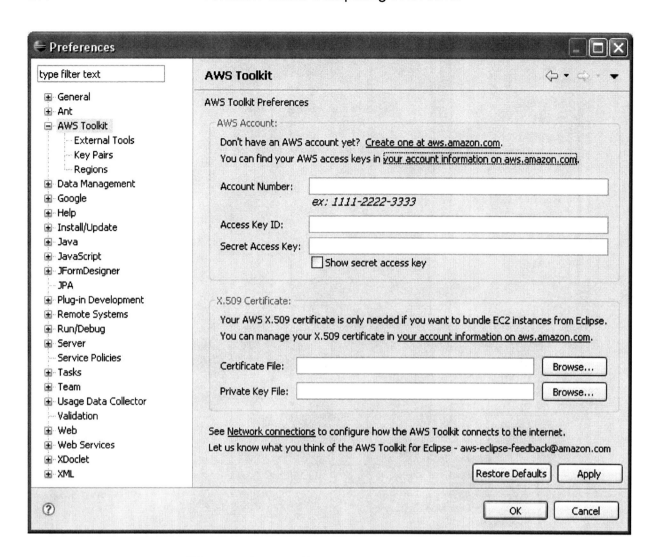

Figure 112 - AWS Toolkit configuration

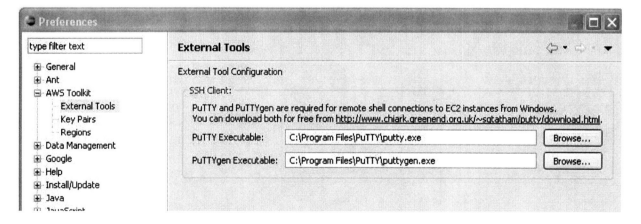

Figure 113 - External Tools Configuration

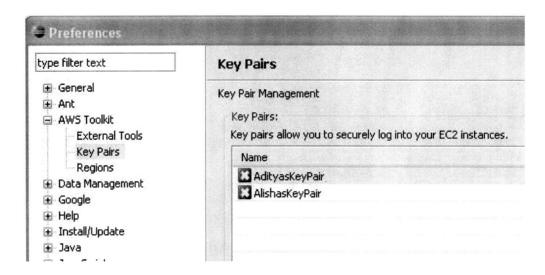

Figure 114 - Configure Key Pairs

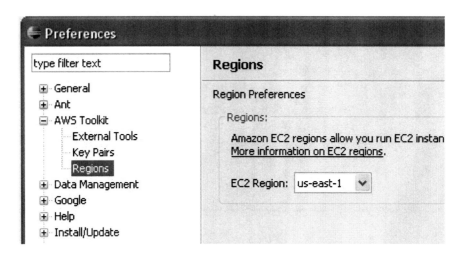

Figure 115 - Regions Configuration

Create the runtime configuration

In the Servers view right click->New->Server and select Amazon EC2 Tomcat v6.0 Cluster option as shown below. Click Next. Select the local Tomcat v6.0 installation directory and select JDK1.5.

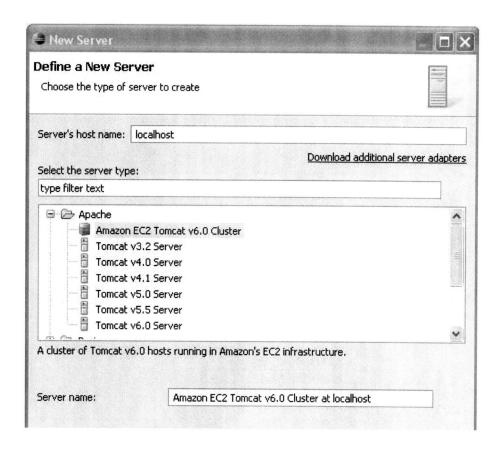

Figure 116 - Define a New Server

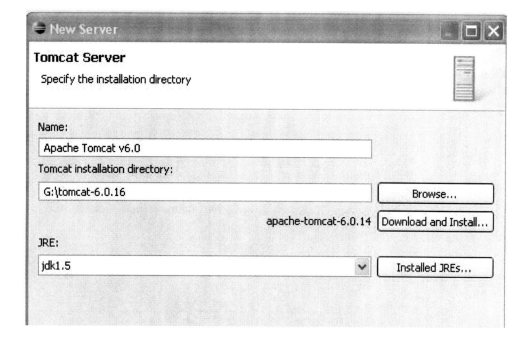

Figure 117 - Select Tomcat Server and JDK

Select the default security group and leave everything at default settings. We don't need an elastic ip for our work so simply click finish. See below.

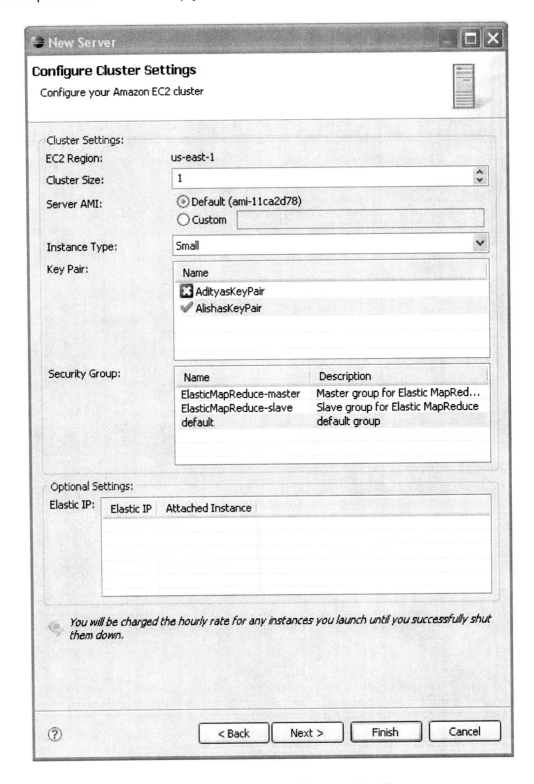

Figure 118 - Configure Cluster Settings

The server shows up in the servers view. Let's start it as it will take about 5 minutes to get ready. Right click on it and click start.

Also create a local Tomcat v6.0 server. We are going to first run our web application on it before running it on AWS.

Create the web application

Create a dynamic web project with the name AWSToolkitDemo as shown and click finish.

Figure 119 - Create Dynamic Web Project

In the WebContent folder create a JSP with the name index.jsp, click next and select the 'New JSP File (xhtml)' template. Open index.jsp and create the following code for it.

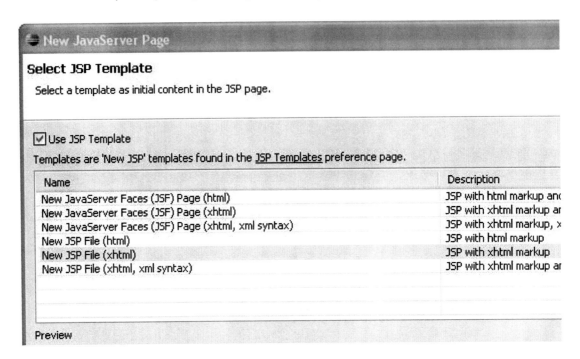

Figure 120 - Select JSP Template

```
index.jsp code listing

<?xml version="1.0" encoding="ISO-8859-1" ?>
<%@ page language="java" contentType="text/html; charset=ISO-8859-1"
    pageEncoding="ISO-8859-1"%>
<!DOCTYPE html PUBLIC "-//W3C//DTD XHTML 1.0 Transitional//EN"
"http://www.w3.org/TR/xhtml1/DTD/xhtml1-transitional.dtd">
<html xmlns="http://www.w3.org/1999/xhtml">
<head>
<meta http-equiv="Content-Type" content="text/html; charset=ISO-8859-1" />
<title>Insert title here</title>
</head>
<body>
<%
String status ="Failure";
if ((request.getParameter("login") !=null) &&
(request.getParameter("login").equals("guest")) &&
    (request.getParameter("password") !=null) &&
(request.getParameter("password").equals("guest"))){
    status="Success";
}
%>
<form id="myform" method="post">
```

```
<%=status %><br/>
Login: <input id="login" name="login" type="text"/><br/>
Password: <input id="password" name="password" type="password"/><br/>
<input type="submit" value="Submit"/>
</form>


</body>
</html>
```

Right click on the server and click add remove projects. Add AWSToolkitDemo project to the server and click finish.

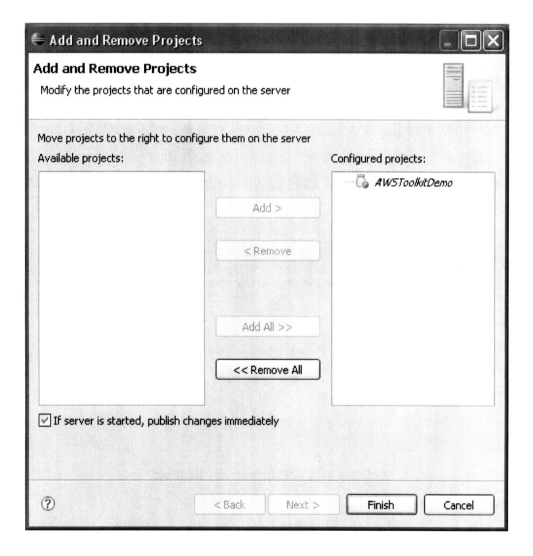

Figure 121 - Add Remove Projects

Right click on index.jsp->Run As->Run On Server. Choose the local tomcat server and click finish. The login page shows up. Enter 'guest' for both login and password and click submit. It shows success. See below.

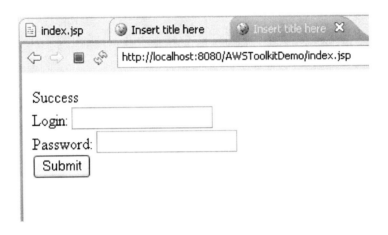

Figure 122 - Success on Localhost

Now click on index.jsp->Run As->Run On Server and select the AWS Tomcat Cluster. The login page shows up again, enter 'guest' for both login and password and click submit. It shows success. Note the URL of the page, it is running on the AWS cloud. See below.

Figure 123 - Success on Cluster

Remote debugging our web application

Lets put a breakpoint in the index.jsp page next to our if statement. We would like to debug the application. To set the break point you have click on the margin beside the code on the left side, at a vertical level that's same as the if statement. See below.

```
<%
String status ="Fa
if ((request.getPa:
    (request.getPa:
    status="Succes:
}
%>
```

Figure 124 - Setting Breakpoint

Right click on the AWS Tomcat Cluster in the servers view and click Restart in Debug. Right click index.jsp->Debug As->Debug On Server and select the AWS Tomcat Cluster. The login page shows up. And eclipse asks if you want to switch to debug perspective. Click yes.

In the variables tab, select the 'status' variable. It shows its value 'Failure'.

Figure 125 - Status Variable in Debug Mode

The server has paused at the if statement. Press F6 to step over one statement at a time.

Managing AMI's Instance's etc.

Click Window->Show View->Other->AWS Toolkit. You will see 4 views. Select all of them and click ok. The views show up at the bottom. Select EC2 Security Groups.

On the left hand side you can manage groups and on the right hand side you can manage permissions in a security group that's selected on the left hand side. See below.

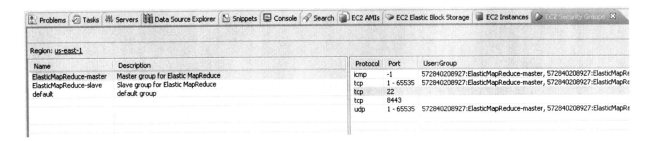

Figure 126 - EC2 Security Groups View

Select the EC2 instances view. You can reboot/terminate instances, bundle them as AMI's, open a remote shell to them giving you root access. See below

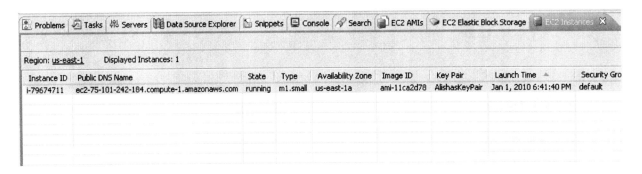

Figure 127 - EC2 Instances View

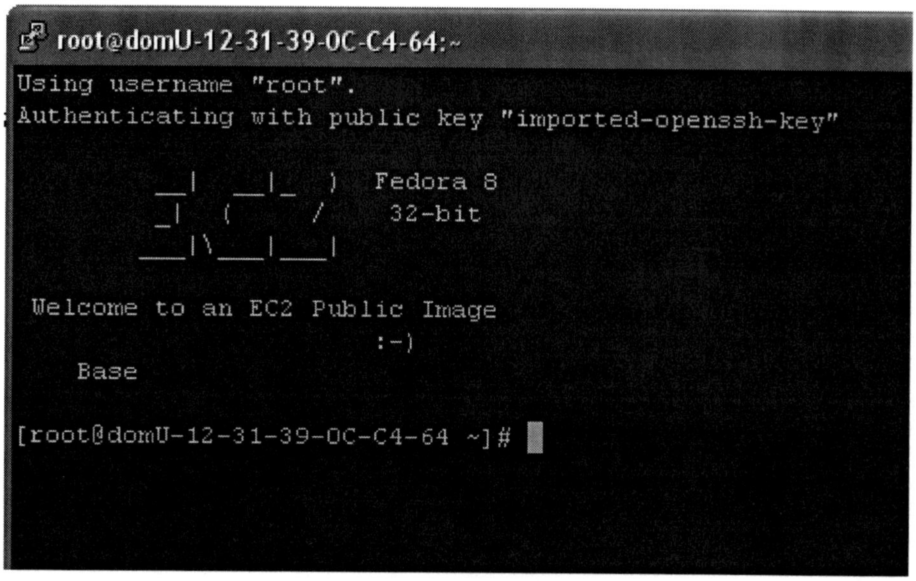

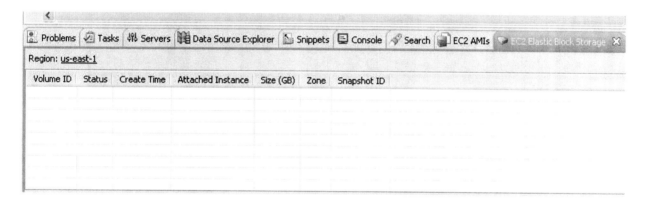

Figure 128 - Remote Shell to the Server

Open the EC2 Elastic Block Storage, you can create/manage volumes, attach/detach them and release them from here. See below.

Figure 129 - EC2 Elastic Block Storage View

Open the EC2 AMI's view. You can start instances of AMI's from here. See below.

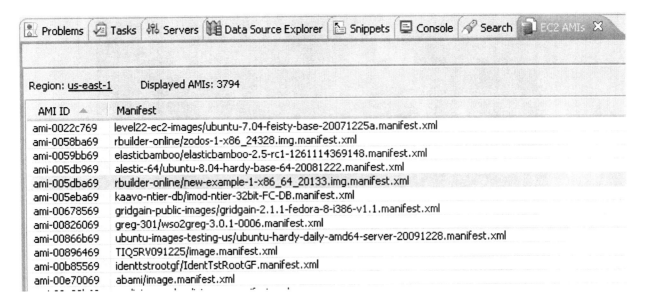

Figure 130 - EC2 AMIs View

Shutdown the remote AWS tomcat cluster. Confirm in the EC2 instances view to make sure the instances have terminated.

Retrospective

We configured the AWS Toolkit in eclipse with our account credentials and certificates. We created a remote AWS Tomcat Cluster and a local Tomcat Server. We ran the web application on both and debugged remotely. Remote debugging is very slow but it works just like local debugging. We saw the 4 views we can use to manage AMIs, Instances, Volumes and Security Groups.

Appendix A: Further Reading

1. Hadoop, http://hadoop.apache.org/

2. Hive, http://hadoop.apache.org/hive/

3. Pig, http://hadoop.apache.org/pig/

4. MySQL, http://www.mysql.com/

5. Apache Ant, http://ant.apache.org/

6. BouncyCastle, http://www.bouncycastle.org/

7. Getting Started with AWS Eclipse Toolkit http://aws.amazon.com/eclipse/

CPSIA information can be obtained at www.ICGtesting.com
Printed in the USA
LVOW031918240212

270297LV00004B/73/P